Up North
St. Louis's Summer Colonies on Lake Huron
in the Golden Age of Travel

Up North

St. Louis's Summer Colonies on Lake Huron in the Golden Age of Travel

Douglas Scott Brookes

Missouri History Museum
St. Louis
Distributed by University of Chicago Press

For
Agnes Greene Brookes
1883-1961

A true devotee of
Gratiot Beach
if ever there was one

Library of Congress Cataloging-in-Publication Data
Brookes, Douglas Scott, 1950-
  Up north : St. Louis's summer colonies on Lake Huron in the golden age of travel
/ Douglas Scott Brookes.
      p. cm.
  Includes bibliographical references and index.
  Summary: "Focusing on the popularity of Lake Huron beaches with St. Louisans
between 1880 and 1950, Up North brings together local newspaper columns and
excerpts from letters and diaries to paint a vivid portrait of life at these summer resorts. Douglas Scott Brookes weaves together his family's experiences with the larger
story of the rise of vacationing in America"--Provided by publisher.
  ISBN 978-1-883982-74-4 (pbk. : alk. paper)
1. Huron, Lake, Region (Mich. and Ont.)--Social life and customs--19th century
2. Huron, Lake, Region (Mich. and Ont.)--Social life and customs--20th century. 3.
Saint Louis (Mo.)--Social life and customs--19th century. 4. Saint Louis (Mo.)--Social
life and customs--20th century. 5. Vacations--Huron, Lake, Region (Mich. and Ont.)-
-History--20th century. I. Missouri History Museum, issuing body.
II. Title.
  F572.H92B76 2013
  977.8'66--dc23
                                    2013006965

Cover photo by Daniel C. Krummes
Back cover photo by Daniel C. Krummes and Mary Scott Brookes
Printed and bound in the United States by Sheridan Books
Distributed by University of Chicago Press

Contents

When at the beach she first appeared, she wore an air of gloom,
And after this for three long days she did not leave her room.

Oh, was this maiden ill? Not so. She did not care to roam
Until they came. For she had left—her curling tongs at home.

—Anonymous (July 14, 1894)

Introduction

Along with generations of my St. Louis family, every summer of my life but two—and those two were mistakes—I have spent at the old family cottage along the shores of southern Lake Huron at its namesake town of Port Huron, Michigan. One chilly day there in 2005, puttering through drawers, I came across the diary that Ada Greene, my father's grandmother, kept from 1911 to 1915. In simple words, in her cursive hand and spelling and phrasing from a bygone age, Ada recorded everyday life during summers in those years before World War I, in her wooden cottage along what is still known as Gratiot Beach (pronounced GRĂ-shut). In Ada's day Gratiot Beach designated the lakefront line, two-thirds of a mile long, of privately owned summer cottages, punctuated midway by the rambling Windermere Hotel. At its southern end, the neighboring resort of Huronia Beach (pronounced Hyoo-ROH-niya) bustled with families who had opted to rent their bit of summer heaven, among the tightly packed row of wooden cottages that for three months each year offered the same cooling breezes off shimmering Lake Huron, the passing parade of steamers and barges and sailing yachts, and the forested shoreline of Canada disappearing below the horizon to the east, all under the ethereal blue of the Michigan summer sky.

Reading Ada's words proved pleasant for the descriptions of life she drew, and was also a way to meet this "Grandmother Greene" (as my father fondly spoke of her) whom I'd never known. Easy enough.

But then Ada's tales of summer life so long ago began to shadow my days. Gratiot Beach, the Windermere Hotel, Huronia (the latter two long gone)—so vibrant in Ada's words, now their stories seemed lost. The lake still shimmers in summer sunshine, yes, but the teeming resorts of the diary have disappeared, matured like wild children grown up and old, transfigured somehow into today's sedate row of year-round homes, quiet unless a firecracker punctuates midsummer, peaceful unless the lake kicks up a storm, provincial as city dwellers imagine a Michigan town must be. Had all those people really come *here*, and just for the summer? Even my father, who spent the happiest days of his life at Gratiot, began in his last years to doubt there'd ever really been such a place as Huronia Beach, as though his memory were tricking him. But Ada's diary, and other family diaries that surfaced later, would have reassured him, had he lived to read them. So would the stacks of family letters, tied in pink ribbon by the caring hand of my grandmother Agnes, Ada's daughter, telling a happy story in the delighted and hurried tones of vacationers, whom duty compelled to address the poor suckers stuck back home in the stultifying heat of St. Louis or Cincinnati. So too the amateur, sepia photographs, in albums whose brittle black pages have begun to crack, my grandmother's white pencil lovingly recording (some forty years later, no doubt in the depths of a St. Louis winter) who the long-ago frolickers in scratchy-looking bathing outfits were, where that charming cottage with the fluted porch columns stood, when that steamer sailed down the St. Clair River. Ever practical, Agnes kept her captions strictly functional. MOTHER, 1908. HOT WEATHER. Occasionally she waxed whimsical. ME, NOT SULKING, ONLY WITH TOOTHACHE. And WHY THE PENSIVE LOOK, DR. CARLISLE?

Reading the letters and diaries was like putting in a telephone line to the long-dead merrymakers in the photographs. They were talking again. Maybe their words could reveal the secret that made their faces beam with

The author's great-grandparents, Will and Ada Greene, at the Port Huron train station, 1908.

wonder, or gaze serenely, even gratefully, as though something about the lazy summer days at the beach had bathed them in bliss.

And so, as one might guess, the simple reading of a small diary morphed into the gigantic project of unearthing the forgotten story of summering at Huronia and Gratiot beaches, from the beginning (if documents would reveal when that was), until the 1950s, by which time Huronia Beach had long since disappeared, the Windermere Hotel was toast (it burned down), and most of Gratiot's cottages had been knocked down or recast into year-round homes. When did all this summering start? Why here? Who came, and how? What brought the whole grand cavalcade to a shattering end, and when? Most engagingly of all, what was life like at these summer resorts in that age before computers, or television, or even radio?

The book in your hand is the result. It uses those family diaries and letters, as well as the reminiscences my father fondly put down on paper decades later, but also the rich trove of beach columns in the Port Huron newspapers, to tell the story of Americans loafing away summers at cottage resorts—in this case, at the twin Michigan magnets that drew midwestern city dwellers by the trainload each summer, including sweltering St. Louisans.

To be sure, St. Louisans flocked to western Michigan resorts as well, but through-sleeper train service ensured that plenty flooded into Huronia and Gratiot Beaches at the eastern tip of the state. Nor was St. Louis the only city represented here; as we shall see, Cincinnati and Columbus beat St. Louis to the site, then Detroiters swamped the resorts once that city boomed. But in the Golden Age of travel before World War I—when, as hindsight makes clear, Michigan resorts reached their pinnacle of popularity—the Mound City reigned supreme as Queen of Lake Huron Beaches. The resorts popped up so frequently in the *St. Louis Post-Dispatch* society columns that often as not the paper omitted the tag, "Michigan;" everyone who was anyone in St. Louis knew where "Huronia Beach" and "Gratiot Beach" were without specifying the state.

Why—the question should be asked—devote such effort to uncovering the story of summer revelers in one small midwestern lakeside town, a veritable flyspeck on the map of America? Especially since the tale of people with means apparently frittering away their summer days does not seem, at first glance, a critically important topic for understanding, say, the broad sweep of American history. But with just a bit of reflection it soon becomes apparent that the story of summering along Lake Huron fits into the larger social phenomenon that began to spread widely among the American middle class in the 1870s: taking a summer vacation at a resort. And that taking that vacation was important to these people. It wasn't just a mindless diversion. It formed a critical part of their year. Arguably *the* critical part. They looked forward to it all winter. They became somehow different people as they boarded the train or boat or, later, the automobile that transported them to their summer paradise. They delighted in their days at the resort, freed from routine: from housekeeping to a degree (at least, if you rented your cottage), from school, from work. Their social lives peaked during these warm summer days. More than a few sought, and found, future mates among their fellow resorters. When the time came to end their vacation, they did so with great regret. They savored its delights not only over the winter, but for the rest of their lives. Their summer migrations even added a new word and phrase to the English language: *beacher* and *the Beach colony*.

Besides, even though only a small percentage of American families down the decades has actually owned a cottage or vacationed in one, the idea of the summer cottage has to a large degree formed our culture's notion of what the ideal summer holiday should be.[1]

Summer Vacations in American Culture

Summering in this corner of water-blessed Michigan derives directly from the larger story of Americans On Vacation, a tale that reaches back to the health spas for wealthy Americans in colonial days. But travel for relaxation didn't spread among the American populace until the confluence of two factors: the rise of the middle class, especially the upper middle class, which could afford the travel in both time and money, and the construction of the ever vaster railroad network that made quick travel over long distances feasible. These two factors joined forces by around 1850, stimulating the phenomenon of summer leisure touring, and tweaking the word *vacation* to mean not just school holiday but travel for pleasure.[2]

The new fad clearly struck a willing chord. Recreational travel by the emerging middle class grew markedly in the 1850s, suffered only a slight and temporary setback during the Civil War, and truly boomed after 1870. The earlier health spas for the rich were now joined by a mushrooming array of summer destinations for the middle class, destinations easily accessible, relatively speaking, thanks to the expanding railroad and steamer lines linking the country together. After all, if one could afford it, who wouldn't jump at the chance to escape the heat and noxious fumes of the cities, savoring instead the change of air and pace, and the amusing fun far from home and its routines? And since North American schools typically emptied out all summer long, if one were traveling with youngsters why not plan on leaving town for weeks, even months, if finances allowed, until school opened again in September?[3]

The vacationing trend only accelerated in the 1880s and 1890s, in all corners of the country that offered seashore, lakeshore, mountain scenery, or mineral springs capable of attracting customers. In the lakeshore department Michigan held a rich hand to play, and quickly emerged to lead the boom as soon as its entrepreneurs caught wind of the trend.

In the variety of accommodations offered, the new resorts reflected the wide gamut of human tastes, from primitive to extravagant. Some holiday spots kept themselves strictly religious in focus, others indulged in the vices, notably drinking and gambling. Still others—the vast majority of resorts across America—positioned themselves in the middle ground as "respectable" family destinations, meaning suitable for married couples with children, or single ladies, and offering a standard of accommodation and fare that avoided the extremes of either rough camp or luxury hotel. By no means religious retreats, they nonetheless welcomed, even courted, church-going customers and might provide a chapel for Sunday worship, all the while remaining undogmatic enough to include card-playing and dancing among the entertainments—diversions usually banned at strictly religious camps. At the same time, as part of keeping "respectable" no alcohol would be offered in the dining hall or sold on the grounds of these family-oriented retreats.

In other words, the family resorts—of which Huronia and Gratiot Beaches formed two examples—sought to attract the middle-class householder on the lookout for a reliable, secular summer haven that would shock neither pocketbook nor prevailing social values. The potential sojourner here wasn't looking to follow high-society fashion as at Mackinac Island's Grand Hotel, for example, the fellow Michigan resort that opened seven years after Huronia and two after Gratiot. In fact the lure of the middle-ground resorts lay largely in the simplicity of the cottages and hotels. There was something liberating about forsaking the pampering amenities of home in favor of Spartan wooden walls and plain furniture, at least for a few weeks.

Yet cottagers did want to be comfortable, and safe, and they were definitely looking for amusement. Or, better said, recreation, as American culture since the days of the Puritans had looked askance at overlong indulgence in pure diversion. And so we see Huronia and Gratiot, as exemplars of middle-class family resorts, offering plenty of amusement and recreation, mixed in with educational and cultural offerings that sought to elevate the mind, even on summer vacation. The educational uplift would temper the natural human tendency, when freed from normal routine, to just plain goof off. America, with its unrelenting stress on hard work and advancement, approved.

But let us not take the country's work and self-improvement ethic too seriously. After all, part of the attraction of summer holidays for adults lay in the chance to act more freely than at home, rather like a child again.[4] As the following pages attest, resorters were clearly looking for fun, so that in the 1880s and 1890s they quickly embraced the growing national fascination with team games including baseball, softball, bowling, and tennis, and the true craze that emerged in these decades, bicycling. One might read this indulgence in sport as complementing nicely the devotion to work and self-improvement in the national psyche. Another motive loomed behind the sport of it all, for part of the attraction of resort games lay in the fact that men and women on vacation could participate in sports together far more readily than society of the day might permit back home. Indeed a novelty of resorts lay in women's very participation in sports that were largely reserved for men at home.[5]

No doubt about it, something about the closed, safe world of the resort chipped away at societal barriers still very much in vogue in the world outside. Here at the summertime seaside (or in our case, lakeside) there reigned "a new kind of emotional space, an experimental zone," in the words of cultural historian Orvar Löfgren.[6] Society's rules still stood, to be sure, but they could be bent a bit, and wasn't that the point of summer vacation: to spend time as *you* wished, within reason, not as work or school or home dictated, or even, if one could get away with it, as society demanded? Away from home and its conventions, you could try your hand at different activities, even different behaviors.

Along with daytime play, so in evenings too men and women spent far more time in each other's company than at home, in the soirees and dances the resorts offered. Surely this constituted the greatest draw of resorts, at least for the unattached (and no doubt for some of the attached), as young hearts fluttered at the thought of whom they might meet that summer. Mother and Dad might be coming to get away from it all, but their unmarried offspring were hoping, likely as not, to get into it all.

In fact, most resorters weren't looking to get away from people, or they would have chosen an isolated farmhouse or cabin or mountain camp for their vacation rather than a bustling resort with cottages quite close together, as at Huronia and Gratiot. No, they wanted to mingle, with the kind of people who shared their values, by and large. Soon enough, summering at the right faraway resort evolved into one hallmark of social success among the middle class—a hallmark newspapers were quick to trumpet in summer society columns.

And so these new summer resorts caught on dramatically, thanks to the potent mix of escape they offered: to milder climate and cleaner air, to new and inspiring vistas, new friends, new routines based largely on personal choice, to fun, to amusement—all coupled with the exciting prospect of stretching society's rules a bit. And as waterside resorts quickly demonstrated, nary a better tool has existed for stretching society's rules than the swimming suit at a crowded beach.

In the trickle and then flood of visitors in the new phenomenon of summer tourism, then, beach-blessed Michigan rather quickly found itself a hot item. Hitherto remote and neglected lakefront villages and towns scrambled to attract and absorb the swelling summer influx, turning their previously unheralded waterside bounties into dollar makers, at least for three or four months out of the year. Of this new summer industry Port Huron's Huronia and Gratiot Beach resorts served as early and typical examples.

The other side of the coin was, of course, the town and the repercussions the resorts worked upon it, a theme popping up frequently in the following pages alongside the goings-on at the resorts themselves. If Port Huron's experience serves as a gauge, we can say that by and large America's resort towns developed a positive, smiling relationship with their seasonal visitors. One might have thought it a love/hate relationship. After all, the cottagers and tourists pumped dollars into the local economy and provided jobs in the hotels and cottages, yes, and plenty of them were decent people, plus their annual arrival heralded the welcome start of summer. But these loafing outsiders didn't really share local concerns, they existed in a completely different "on vacation" frame of mind, no doubt some turned up their noses at the natives (except where Cupid's bow was involved), and then they ran out of town when the hard weather set in. Yet nothing in the Port Huron newspapers or family correspondence reveals resentment by the locals (except, again, where Cupid's bow figured in, and that only rarely). Instead the townies were practical and welcoming of the annual injection of new life—and dollars—into the local scene.

In adjusting itself each year to the seasonal flood of vacationers, modest Port Huron and similar resort towns unwittingly followed the path blazed by swanky Nice, the French Riviera destination that in the early nineteenth century became among the world's first "to organize itself to meet the needs of a powerful alien group with no wish to fit into local life."[7] Romantics might invoke the mellow midwestern temperament to explain its easy adjustment, but whatever the reason, the Michigan city adapted itself quite smoothly to the seasonal incoming throngs. Unlike Nice with its hordes of international tourists, the fact that American resort towns catered to fellow Americans and Canadians who all spoke the same language (more or less) no doubt accounted for much of the smooth accommodation.

And so Huronia and Gratiot Beaches fit neatly into the version of vacationing that flourished among families of moneyed (yet not ostentatiously wealthy), white, Protestant (with a few Catholic) businessmen and professionals in America's upper middle class, in the last three decades of the nineteenth century and first two of the twentieth. Yet by the middle of the twentieth century, the resort phenomenon already showed signs of decided decline. What brought the curtain down on the age of family summer resorts, including Huronia and Gratiot, so relatively soon after it all began?

In Huronia's case the default of the owner on loans accelerated its closure, but without doubt Huronia too, as did Gratiot and the three summer hotels here, would have fallen victim soon enough to the economic and social developments that connived against traditional summertime resorts all over the country. Leading the attack was the 1930s Depression, along with the rises in labor and other costs particularly after World War II, both of which exacerbated the perennial difficulty of operating a resort in a climate that can attract customers at best only four or five months out of the year. Add to that the spread of good roads and reliable automobiles, and plenty of hotels and then motels and auto camps practically everywhere, so that after 1935 or so families and individuals with the means to do so could opt for summer touring about the country rather than plunking down in one spot for weeks or even months on end. Paradoxically, though, middle-class mothers were now working more and more outside the home, which further decreased the number of families with children who could settle down in vacation cottages or hotels for long stints.

Added to the improved infrastructure that made touring around the country feasible, the advent of inexpensive airline travel in the 1950s brought even once-exotic foreign lands within reach of the resorts' traditional clientele, further siphoning off patronage. And so tastes in vacationing simply shifted. Compared to motor trips out West or flying off to Europe, settling in for weeks at an aging lakeside resort in Michigan began to seem decidedly passé. Great Lakes passenger steamers—resorts with propellers— faced the same gang of goblins.

Into this new age the old summer holiday spots fit uneasily. The grand old resort hotels soldiered on, fueled by the group tourist trade. But cottage resorts in the traditional mold, including Huronia and Gratiot Beaches and their three hotels, largely disappeared from the American scene. Exceptionally, the odd resorter holdouts doggedly carry on the private family cottage tradition amid year-round homes, like nomads migrating to summer pastures full of natives.

Among all of the regions cashing in on the emerging resort industry across the country, ironically for Michigan the state's natural beauties sparked the rise of cottage resorts, but then some forty years later the state's automobile industry pummeled them into a quaint obsolescence.

Notes on the Sources

With the exceptions noted below, newspaper quotes dated 1909 or earlier are from the *Port Huron Daily Times*, while those dated 1910 and later are from its successor, the *Port Huron Times Herald*. In the text, the date of the newspaper excerpt appears within parentheses following the quote.

For quotations from all other sources, the following abbreviations after the date indicate the source (the family letters, diaries, and monographs noted below are largely in the collections of the Missouri History Museum Library and Research Center, St. Louis).

ADG: correspondence of Ada D. Greene (1851–1939), Pittsburgh, and Salem, Ohio, wife of William S. ("Will") Greene, mother of Clarence, Agnes, and Clark Greene; cottage owner at Gratiot from 1902 until her death.

ADGdiary: diary of Ada D. Greene at Gratiot Beach, 1911–1915

AGB: correspondence of Agnes G. Brookes (1883–1961), Pittsburgh and (after September 1911) St. Louis, daughter of Ada Greene, wife of Theodore P. Brookes, M.D.

H: *Port Huron Daily Herald*

HSB: correspondence of Henry S. Brookes, M.D. (1858–1939), St. Louis, father of Theodore

JIB: diary of Jean I. Brookes, Ph.D. (1898–1988), St. Louis, daughter of Henry S. and Mary P. Brookes, in the year 1914 while at Huronia Beach; for other years, her correspondence

KG: *Kalamazoo Gazette*

MF: *Michigan Farmer*

MPB: correspondence of Mary P. Brookes (1859–1948), St. Louis, wife of Henry S. Brookes, M.D., mother of Theodore

RDB: correspondence of Robert D. Brookes, M.D. (1913–2000), St. Louis, son of Theodore and Agnes

RDB Huronia: personal reminiscence of Robert D. Brookes, M.D., entitled "Huronia," composed circa 1987

SC: *The Sunday Commercial* newspaper, published at Port Huron

SLPD: *St. Louis Post-Dispatch*

TPB: correspondence of Theodore P. Brookes, M.D. (1887–1948), St. Louis, son of Henry S. and Mary P. Brookes, husband of Agnes

TPBJr: correspondence of Theodore P. Brookes, Jr. (1912–1990), St. Louis, son of Theodore and Agnes

Remarks within parentheses appear as such in the original texts. Remarks within brackets are mine. Spelling and capitalization have been retained as they appear in the original.

Acknowledgments

Heartfelt thanks to my good friend Edward R. Moore, Jr., resident on the shores of Lake Huron some seventy years, for his dogged research that made so many of the annotations possible, and for his ever-positive attitude toward life. Longtime Gratioters Jennie Holekamp Burst and Jane Peters shared their memories with me, and for their kindness I am grateful.

Thanks also to the helpful staff at the St. Clair County Public Library in Port Huron, as well as the county's Register of Deeds office. Since Port Huron's city hall burned down in 1949, taking building records with it in the flames, reconstruction of when structures came and went at the town's resorts has relied on sleuth work in the Library and Deeds Office instead, and in many cases cannot be established.

The family letters and diaries quoted in the text speak a great deal of Ada Greene's daughter Agnes and son-in-law Theodore Brookes, my father's parents. Agnes, from Pittsburgh but finishing her education at St. Margaret's College in Toronto, and Theodore, just out of medical school and escaping steamy St. Louis with his parents to spend summers as a kind of doctor-on-call at Huronia, numbered among the couples who met each other in Lake Huron summer romances. In 1911 they married up north, in Ada's cottage at Gratiot.

All three appear frequently in these pages. Ada and her son-in-law Theodore left this earth before I could know them, but by the time I knew my grandmother Agnes in the 1950s, she had evolved into a sensible, colorful, bespectacled, full-figured, arthritic, intelligent elderly lady who tinted her hair pure white, always wore dresses (as a lady did in those days) and sensible white shoes, walked cautiously with an aluminum cane, conducted herself with dignity, attended church regularly, did not suffer fools, and wrote in a bold, slanting hand in green ink from her scratchy fountain pen. She loved Port Huron to the depths of her soul, simply waiting out winters in St. Louis until she could return to "the Beach," as she called it, always willing to

Agnes Greene ("not sulking, only with tooth-ache") and her fiancé, Theodore Brookes, M.D., Port Huron train station, September 1908.

jump into the Oldsmobile and race down Gratiot Avenue (plate of breakfast waffles on her lap, if need be) to savor yet one more time the passenger steamer *South American* gliding majestically under the Blue Water Bridge of a sunny Friday morning. How wonderful to read in these pages of Agnes as an energetic young girl playing tennis and paddling canoes.

But most of all, I lovingly pause to celebrate my partner, Daniel Krummes. A native Californian, he didn't know what to expect when he first saw Gratiot Beach in 1978, but soon fell under its spell, becoming a Michigander at heart. While he did not live to see it in print, his steadfast support through the research and writing made this book possible. It is more for him than for anyone.

Douglas Scott Brookes
November 2012

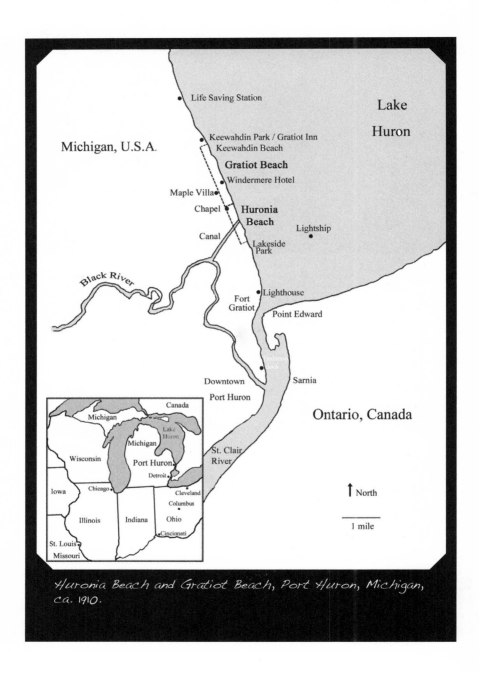

Life Saving Station

Lake
Huron

Michigan, U.S.A.

Keewahdin Park / Gratiot Inn
Keewahdin Beach

Gratiot Beach

Windermere Hotel

Maple Villa

Chapel   **Huronia
Beach**

Canal

Lightship

Lakeside
Park

Black River

Fort
Gratiot

Lighthouse

Point Edward

Downtown
Port Huron

Sarnia

Ontario, Canada

Canada

Michigan

Lake
Huron

Michigan

Wisconsin

Port Huron

St. Clair
River

Detroit

Iowa   Chicago

Cleveland
Columbus

Illinois   Indiana   Ohio

Cincinnati

St. Louis

Missouri

↑ North

1 mile

*Huronia Beach and Gratiot Beach, Port Huron, Michigan,
ca. 1910.*

Chapter 1

Summer Loafing, Lake Huron Style

The fine tradition of lazing away summer days on the shores of southern Lake Huron at Port Huron, Michigan, got its start in 1879, when local entrepreneurs cast an eye on the nearly empty lakeshore just north of town. Loggers had already harvested whatever trees could be felled and farmers had tilled the earth here and there, where soil permitted. Now to what use could enterprising folk put the sandy beach along beautiful Lake Huron? The *Port Huron Daily Times* was quick to sound the clarion call to local businessmen:

> Profit and prosperity await the man who buys a tract of land
> above the lighthouse, or at any other desirable point on the
> shore of Lake Huron or St. Clair River in or near Port Huron,
> builds a good summer hotel, and makes and keeps an attractive
> summer resort. People are beginning to learn that Port Huron
> has a summer climate as delightful as that to be found in any
> other section of the country. . . . (August 28, 1879)

Prosperity beckoned, and the next year, 1880, entrepreneurs cleared away brush for picnickers and bathers along the pristine shores of Lake Huron just north of town and put up the first row of rental cottages. No one bothered that year to name the newly hatched resort, but in July 1881 the newspaper announced that the lakeshore site would hereafter be "Huronia Beach."[8] The paper didn't tell who coined the pleasing name, so appropriate for Lake Huron, but fingers point to Marcus Young, the energetic Port Huron entrepreneur and land agent. For more than anyone, Mr. Young got the idea for a resort going—literally, when in 1881 he began running his canvas-topped omnibus (horse-drawn stagecoach) complete with "cushioned side seats," so his ads touted, from Fort Gratiot—the old village where Lake Huron empties into the St. Clair River, just above Port Huron—past the city's new Lakeside Cemetery, and up to the lonely beach just north of the woods that later became the town's Lakeside Park.

At its start the nascent resort amounted to no more than a tiny dot of activity on the otherwise empty lakeshore:

> "Lost on Huronia Beach" was the fate of a party of ladies the other evening. They engaged a carriage and started for the beach where they intended to spend the evening. The ride was very pleasant until they reached the woods when they lost their way, and were unable to get on the right track. For several hours they wandered in and out among the trees on the lonely shore, somewhat frightened by the moaning of the trees and the roaring of the waves. (August 26, 1881)

From these modest beginnings Mr. Young spent the rest of his life managing the resort he owned, promoting it tirelessly to prospective renters in the great cities of the Midwest. He hit his mark among prosperous families looking to flee the stifling heat and dubious air back home to indulge in the new fashion of taking a summer vacation, in this case escaping to rustic cottages along the cool waters of beckoning Lake Huron. In the beginning Mr. Young's marketing efforts succeeded most spectacularly in Cincinnati, Columbus, and Detroit, with smatterings of customers from Kansas City, Louisville, and Toledo. Occasionally Deep Southerners even reached Huronia from Arkansas, Tennessee, Texas, and New Orleans. But as we've seen, in the Beach's heyday from the mid-1890s to the mid-1910s, St. Louis, the nation's fourth-largest city in 1900, surpassed them all, and made Huronia its own.

> Many of the resorters have left the beaches this week for their homes. It is claimed that more people came from St. Louis than from any other place in the United States. (August 19, 1908)

As cottagers flocked to Port Huron's burgeoning lake resorts in record numbers during those years, Huronia and Gratiot took to grandly tagging themselves the "Atlantic City of the Great Lakes" after the great summer destination of the East Coast. Hyperbole aside, Mr. Young's efforts so transformed the northern edge of town that at his death the *Port Huron Times Herald* dubbed him, in its lengthy front-page obituary of August 18, 1913, "the Man Who Made Port Huron's Resorts," and trumpeted that he "Gave His Time, Effort, and Money to Build One of the Greatest Summer Colonies in Michigan."

All this from a resort that by later standards was rather simple, even primitive. Huronia offered modest wooden cottages shoulder-to-close-shoulder in a tidy row facing the lake under the newly planted cottonwood and white birch trees. From the small and screenless front porches one stepped outside the short distance to the broad wooden boardwalk that connected the cottages to one another and to the resort's dining hall and pavilion. Beyond the boardwalk lay the beach and the lake. Not much in the way of lawn at first—mostly sand everywhere, and the first of ongoing struggles to get grass to grow where nature hadn't intended it to.

These rented summer nests were single-story for the most part, of varying sizes but nothing especially large, with parlor and up to four bedrooms,

Huronia Beach, 1905. Twelve feet between cottages still made for close quarters with your neighbor.

Living the Huronia dream. Right: Cottages 39 and 49, 1907. Below: The Pavilion, whose porch doubled as the streetcar stop. Postcard, 1915.

plainly furnished and painted, and no kitchen—"marvels of simplicity," the publicist cheerfully dubbed them. No indoor potty either at first, only an outhouse, probably one behind each cottage, since the city water and sewer lines didn't yet run that far out of town. For the same reason drinking water came by pump straight out of Lake Huron, in those days before pollution concerns.

Already in 1882 the brand-new and still primitive Huronia could charm:

Marcus Young's son Huronia helps his father entice customers, 1906.

The cottage was immediately and unanimously voted "perfectly sweet," "too cute for anything," and is indeed a very bijou of cottages, and furnished with everything needed to make a residence in it delightful. It is two stories in height, with piazza and "Romeo and Juliet" balcony, from which not unfrequently were heard desponding cries for "R-R-R-Romeo!" for the masculine element had been rigorously excluded from the party. (August 15, 1882/MF)

By 1884, four years after it opened, Huronia Beach was a smash hit. That June the *Port Huron Sunday Commercial* newspaper's bombastic article on the Beach, in the style of the day, so fulsomely sang its praises that one suspects the author must have been the ever-resourceful Mr. Young himself:

HURONIA BEACH.
About three miles north of Port Huron, on the sloping shore of Lake Huron, bounded by forest and water and glorious sky and

Idyllic scene at Huronia Beach to make the folks back home envious. Postcard, 1907.

sea, rests lovely Huronia Beach. There where the sturdy Huron warrior and gentle forest maiden whispered words of love, the young man and maiden may walk the strand in peace when the pebbles and water or the ripple glisten in the gloaming. . . . There without recourse to hermit life the man of business may rest, secluded from its excitement and cares and yet in the full flare of all that is going on in all the world . . . [H]e can get his daily paper daily; he can enjoy mail and telephone facilities; he can take a train for north, south, east, or west, at almost any hour of the twenty-four; he can board a steamboat for any lake port almost any moment; or he can sail, or row, or swim, or fish in the grandest of water; or he can stroll in a primeval forest, untouched by desecrating hand since creation's morn . . . ; the perfect conveniences are all that heart could wish, and here the tired mother sees the humdrum of house-keeping reduced to its simplest form and going along smoothly while she may rest. (June 2, 1884)

To which one can only add, "Oh, brother."

Enter Gratiot Beach

Growing up in St. Louis during the school year, I'd join my family for the occasional trip downtown to the broad cobblestone levee that, we were told, slaves had built along the Mississippi River. It was the closest we could come in landlocked Missouri to what we missed: the vast blue horizon of Lake Huron that soothed the eyes, freed the imagination, and challenged the lucky sod standing on its shore to dream. As the plodding Mississippi towboats nudged their barges along the rusty river—poor substitutes, in our eyes, for the dashing Great Lakes freighters—the distant blue lake called to us across the farmlands of Illinois and Indiana. But we couldn't answer—at least not until school let out the next June.

On one such trip downtown, in my young teens, a small street sign under the railroad overpass above the levee startled me by announcing "Gratiot." What a coincidence, that un-Michigan St. Louis also had a road named Gratiot, just like Port Huron! A teenager may be forgiven for ignorance about Charles Gratiot, of the early St. Louis mercantile family, West Point class of 1806. The young engineer and army officer designed the fort at the foot of Lake Huron that later bore his name. In its turn the fort passed that moniker onto the summer haven to which trainloads of Mr. Gratiot's fellow St. Louisans would flock a century later, no doubt also blissfully unaware of its St. Louis connection.

Mr. Gratiot's namesake resort of Gratiot Beach was born just five years after Huronia, its neighbor to the south. Huronia's success clearly inspired the development of Gratiot, but as private summer homes (and one hotel), rather than as a communal resort where customers rented the cottages and management fed and entertained them.

By late 1884 the lakefront land immediately north of Huronia—called at first "Brighton Beach" after the famed resort on England's south coast—belonged entirely to Charles Ward, the well-to-do Port Huron banker and grain dealer who had also invested in Huronia. Figuring he could turn a profit somehow, what with Huronia bulging with summer folk next door, Mr. Ward purchased Brighton Beach from its various local owners and then readied his new waterside kingdom for sale. The next spring, of 1885, he subdivided the land into fifty-nine lots, each fifty feet wide, beginning with Lot #1 at the southern end of the plat. The lots extended 300 feet from the dirt road down toward, but not reaching, the lake, the idea being that the beach itself would be the property of . . . well, that was not quite clear yet, as we shall see. By not extending ownership down to the lake, so reasoning went, no lot owners could build fences or anything else on the beach that would detract from it and harm property values.[9]

That same year Mr. Ward opened the lots for sale to the public. By the time of the sale he'd changed the plat's name to the more Michigan-sounding "Gratiot Beach," after the old army fort that still stood then where Lake Huron narrows into the St. Clair River. With the asking price of $200 per lot, which would gross him nearly $11,000 if all fifty-four lots sold (he had retained five lots for his own use), Mr. Ward stood to reap a grand profit indeed over the $1,600 he had paid for the land.

In summer and fall 1885 the first lots sold. Two adjacent lots, just above the soon-to-be-built Windermere Hotel, went to Port Huron businessman and former mayor Henry Howard, one of the hotel's investors. Five other lots, adjacent to one another toward the southern end of Gratiot Beach, nearest to Huronia and town, sold to families from Ohio.

Almost certainly the Ohioans were summering at Huronia when they learned of the sale of lots at Gratiot. Cincinnati physician Dr. William H. Taylor bought next to his sister, Mrs. Elizabeth Dean, while Columbus banker John Siebert bought next to his business colleague, Orestes A. B. Senter. Within ten years the Columbus duet of Sieberts and Senters expanded into a quartet as their business partners, Charles Lindenberg and William Scarlett, also built cottages at Gratiot Beach. So did Charles Lindenberg's brother Philip.

People nowadays might blanch at the notion of inviting business associates (or even relatives) to join them at their holiday spot, but in the late

Cottages, Gratiot Beach, Mich.

The Lindenberg brothers of Columbus, Ohio, built two cottages, "Clarhom" and "Linden" (center and right), side by side at Gratiot Beach around 1891. Ada Greene bought Clarhom in 1902. Postcard, ca. 1898.

nineteenth century at Gratiot and Huronia quite a few families did just that. Vacationing together provided companionship for the families and ensured they'd encounter the proper atmosphere at the holiday homes. Better a known quantity, after all, than risking summer among complete strangers.

And so the private Gratiot Beach was born. It wasn't exactly a raging success at first, with sales quieting down following that first wave; by the time Mr. Ward moved to Chicago four years later, in 1889, of the original fifty-nine lots he had sold but twenty-three. By 1894 his Gratiot Beach syndicate tried pepping up sales with large ads in the local paper offering the unsold lots at $200 each. This had been the same price as in 1885, nine years earlier, the ads were careful to tout, although they neglected to mention that due to deflation, $200 in 1894 was worth *more* than it had been in 1885, so the syndicate wasn't exactly losing on the deal. The offer was timely, and business brisk.

Who bought the lots in 1894? Well-heeled renters at Huronia, for one, mostly from Ohio and Missouri, looking for larger and more comfortable cottages of their own along the lake. Well-off townsfolk in booming Port Huron also jumped into the summer-cottage craze, purchasing lots and building cottages at Gratiot for their own families or to resell at profit.

As cottages went up, the subsequently familiar tension among lot owners arose as to just how far toward the lake one could extend one's front stoop without offending the neighbors. Truly, "control of territory is thus a touchy issue in cottage cultures."[10]

> The name of Keewahdin Beach should be changed to Zig Zag
> Beach. . . . Each builder seems to have tried to outstrip his
> neighbor by building out a little nearer the beach instead of
> maintaining the line. (July 10, 1900)

Since surviving photographs from the early era are black and white, we'd be left to wonder what colors the early cottages at Gratiot were painted, if the paper hadn't told us:

> The prevailing color of paint along the beach line of cottages is
> green. At the south of Lakeside a cottage in brightest red is an
> innovation which looks well. (May 31, 1902)

Once you'd settled in, wouldn't you want to join the nineteenth-century tradition of naming your cottage? Most owners at Gratiot christened their abodes, and so did wittier renters at Huronia (where cottages were known officially by number), even if just for the summer. Those who did could breathe a sigh of relief to learn that:

> Nearly all of the numerous suggestive titles which were given
> to Huronia cottages last season have remained intact during the
> winter and will greet the returning cottagers. (May 26, 1900)

Clever names at Huronia included Beat It Inn, C'est Vrai, Dewey (during the Spanish-American War), Doo Drop Inn, Kill Care, Knatty Nook, Sans Souci,

Above: The view from Ada Greene's cottage "The Farm," North Gratiot Beach, 1929. Left: Ada's other cottage, "#16," with its second-floor sleeping porch, in 1902, the year she bought it.

the Blow Out, and the enigmatic UUUU. Gratiot monikers ran from Bide-a-Wee, Bungalow, Hacienda, Lochaven, Rest-a-While, Sunny Slope, and Unter den Linden, to the whimsical if puzzling Moon-G.

All in all, the idea of owning your own cottage was a winner not just in the hearts of cottagers, but in cold financial terms:

> Twenty years ago today the late John W. Porter was selling
> fifty-foot lots at Gratiot beach at two hundred dollars each and
> it was difficult to get buyers. Today the same lots cannot be
> purchased for fifteen hundred dollars. In fact . . . there is now
> no vacant property and nothing on the market. Values have
> increased in a greater ratio along the beaches than at any other
> place in the City of Port Huron. (July 25, 1914)

To be sure, other cottage developments mushroomed along the lakeshore
north and south of Huronia and Gratiot Beaches. But none of these upstarts
came close to upsetting the two *grande dames* from their thrones as the
reigning queens of Lake Huron summer resorts.

In 1945, as World War II ended, and twenty-six years after Huronia
had closed, Gratiot Beach marked its sixtieth anniversary. Some clever soul
remembered this fact, and the newspaper's beach columnist recorded old-
timers' memories in folksy 1940s style:

> Gratiot Celebrates Sixtieth Anniversary
> Maybe you didn't know it but this is anniversary year for Gratiot
> beach. Yes sir . . . folks have been making their summer home
> here for 60 years now. Just think . . . we're traditional!
>
> Sixty years ago people also relaxed in the sunshine of Gratiot
> beach—only 60 years ago things were a little different than they
> are today. There was no electricity—just oil lamps—and conse-
> quently there wasn't much housekeeping done. Housewives just
> gathered up the family and for $5 a week they could eat dinner
> at the very popular Windermere hotel each night . . . plenty of
> steaks too! Of course no evening in a fashionable hotel was quite
> complete without a little dancing even in 1885, so the dining
> room furniture was all pushed down to one end of the hall to
> accommodate the dancers.

Other quaint characteristics of beach life were carrying water up
from the lake . . . riding to town in a horse an' buggy named
"Tally Ho" . . . viewing no grass and few trees and swimming
in the never changing blue Lake Huron . . . Happy anniversary,
Gratiot beach! (August 12, 1945)[11]

Polishing the Beach

From the start, Mr. Young worked hard to improve his baby, Huronia Beach,
to meet the rising expectations of his customers and attract still more of
them.

Right after its first official season he built an icehouse, proudly announced in the *Times* of January 19, 1882, "to hold fifteen cords" of ice
that would surely come in handy the following summer. That year too Mr.
Young announced in the paper that he was completing a laundry building
for the resort. One wonders just what was *in* the laundry building; tubs and
washboards, no doubt, and maybe if the mothers or their maids were lucky,
even a tap with some of that fresh lake water.

The water question proved an ongoing challenge, in the years before
the city stepped in to help. The brand-new resort put in its own windmill to
pump the water "into a tank 30 feet above the ground," so that the *Ft. Gratiot
Sun* of June 3, 1882, could trumpet, "Huronia Beach has water-works of its
own." The windmill mustn't have done its job, though, for two years later
the brochure heralded the "hot air engine" that pumped water up from the
lake. To reassure mothers who must have wondered whether their families
would have to carry water up from the lake in pails, ads claimed, "The cottages are supplied with fine lake water, by hydrants in rear of each."[12] Across
the road, the city's new Lakeside Cemetery got its water the same way—via
a pumping engine down at the lakeshore. Clearly that wouldn't really do for
long for either venue, so in summer 1894 the city extended the water mains
to serve both burgeoning graveyard and blossoming resort.

Alongside these rather prosaic improvements, the dramatic inventions of the late nineteenth and early twentieth centuries found their way to summer holiday spots too. Promoters knew that cottagers might want simplicity, but not backwardness.

Electric light revolutionized resorts as it did everywhere else. When Huronia, Gratiot, and Gratiot's Windermere Hotel first opened, candles, kerosene lamps, and gas would have lit interiors, but by summer 1895 the electric light bulb, perfected by Port Huron's own Thomas Edison, converted the darkness of night into something pretty and festive:

> The poles are being placed for the electric light at the Beaches
> and the grounds will next week be handsomely illuminated.
> (July 20, 1895)

Along with electric light came the other great innovation of the late 1800s, the telephone:

> The Windermere Hotel at Gratiot Beach will be connected with
> the telephone exchange after Friday. (July 6, 1888)

> Huronia Beach is now connected with the telephone exchange.
> (July 9, 1889)

Definitely a boon for communication, these phones, but not all they might be. And thank goodness for "Central," the live operator who connected the calls.

> I went down to telephone for a cleaning woman, but the
> telephone was out of commission at the Hotel. (June 27, 1913/
> ADGdiary)

> Katharine received a phone call at Huronia Dining Hall about six
> o'clock Thursday evening from Mrs. Carpenter, reiterating to "send

> Dr. Brookes at once." I then called her from a phone two cottages
> away from our cottage at Gratiot, but connection was so poor that
> they could not hear me at all, and "Central" had to act as a go-be-
> tween and transmit our messages. (August 9, 1913/TPB)

The telegraph, ubiquitous mode of communication before World War II,
came to the beaches too, of course:

> The Western Union has established an office at the Huronia
> Resort hall. Edson E. Potter is the operator in charge. The office
> is established in place of the telephone of other years. (July 7,
> 1900)

One feature begging for improvement was the potty problem. By the 1880s
most well-off city dwellers would have had indoor toilets in their homes, so
having to revert to Huronia's rustic outhouses must have seemed a tad too
much like roughing it. Of course, if you had to go during the night, rather
than feeling your way outside in the dark you used the chamber pot in
your room. The next morning the pot would be emptied into the outhouse.
Unless you had a maid to do so, older sons in the family traditionally had
the malodorous and unenviable task in the mornings of dumping out the
chamber pots of their parents and younger siblings, a chore they did not
relish.[13] And so, no doubt every cottager went flush with excitement at what
was possibly the greatest advance of all, when outhouses finally went the
way of the gooney bird:

> All the three-room cottages at Huronia have this season been
> enlarged to four-room structures, and all have been provided
> with flush closets. (June 25, 1898)

That huge advance was followed the next year by one of the great unheralded inventions of the nineteenth century, the metal window screen. Screens
had been around for years, it just took Port Huron's resorts a while to take
to the notion:

> In the fitting of the cottages for the season [at Huronia] a large
> amount of rebuilding has been done and 400 window and door
> screens have been used. (June 24, 1899)

Only, not on the porches, at least at Huronia:

> We had a good supper, then sat on the porch until the mosqui-
> tos drove us in, then a little reading, then to bed. (August 9,
> 1914/JIB)

Another unheralded advance of the century was modern hydraulic cement.
The original wooden boardwalks at the Beaches, picturesque in their way
but awfully vulnerable to Michigan weather, gave way to the far more du-
rable material. Prosaic such cement might seem today, but its advent was
newsworthy enough to make the papers:

> Work on the new cement walk . . . is nearly completed at Gra-
> tiot. . . . When the entire line is completed a moonlight walk to
> the beaches will be worth more than ever. (May 17, 1902)

The unstoppable Mr. Young was still improving Huronia two decades after
its founding:

> Every available sleeping place at Huronia was occupied on Fri-
> day night. Marcus Young began today cleaning out his new barn
> opposite Huronia and will furnish the upper portion for sleeping
> places for the balance of the season. (July 23, 1898)

> Marcus Young has started a . . . hennery on his farm and is
> having a splendid success. He has 400 young chickens, some of
> which are very nearly ready for broilers. (June 24, 1899)

The booming resort proved so popular that it easily survived being sliced in
two, when the city dug the Black River Canal right through the heart of Hu-

Left: Ada Greene, ca. 1915. Below: Ada's Gratiot cottage after renovations, 1906.

ronia in 1902. One can imagine Mr. Young's reaction to the idea when the city proposed it, but in the end he had to settle for the 150-foot swath cut right through the Beach to the lake, taking six cottages with it. To make up for the loss, six new cottages went up at Huronia's north end, by the chapel. The location of the new cottages wasn't so desirable because they faced the dirt road alongside the chapel, instead of fronting onto Lake Huron. To see

A header into the Canal —The Canal connects Lake Huron with Black River

The Black River Canal cut Huronia Beach in two after 1902, but at least the footbridge over it offered kids a novel diving platform.

the lake you had to step onto the porch and look off to the right. Nonetheless, they too found willing takers.

Once the canal cut through, a steel footbridge, with wood-planked deck, went up over the new channel to connect Huronia's two halves. To put a positive spin on things, though, now resorters could add a boat ride through the canal, continuing for a sail up Black River, as a novel diversion during their vacation at the Beaches. Blind Ned, whom my father remembered, rented boats and canoes for just this purpose from his large tent along the route.[14]

At its height, then, after all the building and rebuilding, Huronia consisted of sixty cottages along with the dining hall, resort hall, and chapel, on twenty acres of lakefront land. Cottages stood much closer to the lake than do the permanent homes on the site today, the intervening decades having taught valuable lessons on the cycles of water levels on the Great Lakes and the damage winter storms can wreak when the lakes are high.

Boom Times

Mr. Young's hard work at Huronia paid off, as the resort filled up summer after summer.

> It is remarked that every shanty, tent, and cottage along the
> shore is rented. A number of those who are determined to stay
> will bring tents for sleeping accommodations. (July 15, 1899)

The pretty, two-story "Maple Villa" that Mr. Young opened around 1897 as an adjunct to Huronia relieved some of the pressure. Despite its slight drawback of not actually being on the lake—it sat across the road behind Gratiot Beach cottages, amid the maple trees—thanks to its low rates the small inn attracted plenty of customers who didn't mind not having a water view. In the end Maple Villa outlasted both Mr. Young and Huronia itself, soldiering on into the late 1930s.

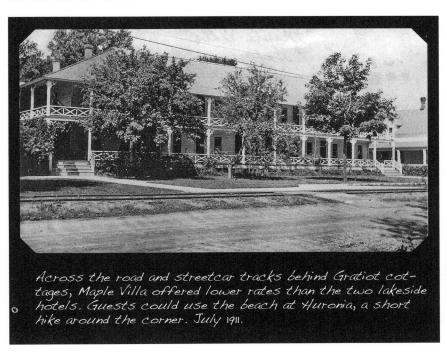

Across the road and streetcar tracks behind Gratiot cottages, Maple Villa offered lower rates than the two lakeside hotels. Guests could use the beach at Huronia, a short hike around the corner. July 1911.

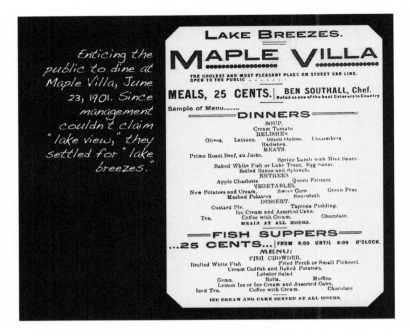

Enticing the public to dine at Maple Villa, June 23, 1901. Since management couldn't claim "lake view," they settled for "lake breezes."

What did vacationers pay at Huronia?

> "How much do your cottages rent for?" asked the reporter.
> "Well," said Mr. Young, "usually from $75 to $100 per month
> will secure a good cottage, all furnished complete. This also
> includes plenty of ice and fuel of all kinds. (August 5, 1892)

Those prices were for the entire cottage, of course, regardless of how many inhabited it, but excluded board since (as we will see) the dining hall operated under separate management from the resort itself. Adding in the $3.50 per person per week the dining hall charged for meals, a month of room and board at Huronia would run a family of five $170. Compare that to the swankiest resorts of the era, which charged $2 to $4.50 a day *per person* for room and board,[15] totaling $300–$675 per month for that family of five. Huronia clearly aimed for the middle class, not the elite. No tipping either at Huronia, where "servants are not allowed to accept fees of any kind"[16]— another plus to the place, for tip-challenged Americans.

Gratiot voguers: Ada Greene with her grandson Clarence, 1908.

How many frolickers did Huronia and Gratiot beaches typically accommodate? From tallies in the town paper, around six hundred at both resorts together, when full.

> At Gratiot Beach not less than 275 people are in the cottages
> and at the Windermere. (August 6, 1898)

> The tables at the Huronia dining hall will all be occupied by
> Monday evening. The hall seats very nearly 300 people at one
> time. (July 13, 1901)

Despite his occasionally overpowering zeal, one must admire the bravado of Mr. Young, the eternal showman:

> First Arrival at Huronia.
> Mr. and Mrs. Marcus Young, of Maple Villa, Huronia Beach,
> are entertaining a fresh arrival at their home, in the person of a
> young son. Marcus is happy, and says the boy's name is "Huro-
> nia." (May 27, 1898)

Chapter 2
The Elegant Windermere

With Huronia Beach raking in customers aplenty, even turning people away, it wouldn't take long for enterprising entrepreneurs to realize they too could cash in on the lucrative seasonal trade by putting up hotels along the evolving lakeshore.

Charles Ward, the Port Huron capitalist who thought up Gratiot Beach, started the hotel ball rolling when he realized he could probably clear a tidy sum with a summer hotel right among the lots he was selling off for private cottages. And so the same year he began offering Gratiot Beach lots for sale, 1885, he set aside four of the lots for his inn. That totaled two hundred feet in which to build. The idea made business sense, and he convinced Port Huron lumbermen Henry Howard and John Sanborn to join him in the venture—both men also building cottages near the site along the Beach and urging others to do the same—along with Marcus Young, whose experience managing the Huronia resort could help get the nascent hostelry up and running.

The new "Ward's Hotel" opened for business in 1886. The plain wooden structure, Dutch Colonial in style thanks to its broad gambrel roof, and probably built of Michigan white pine supplied by Mr. Ward's partners, would not have won awards for architectural beauty. Port Huron's newest hotel frankly resembled a large barn, except for the generous two-story porch facing the lake and the five dormer windows that pierced the roof. Testing the resort waters before plunging in with too large an investment, Mr. Ward kept his hotel smallish, with only sixteen guest chambers, as they called them, and dining room. The hotel must have seemed rather lonely when it opened along Lake Huron, since it shared the entire half-mile stretch of Gratiot Beach with only five brand-new cottages.

In a bid to sound more enticing, the year it opened the establishment acquired its permanent name: *Windermere*, after the pretty lake and tourist

Windermere Hotel, Gratiot Beach

At the barnlike Windermere Hotel, wooden simplicity + good dining + beach and social amenities = typical summer hotel of the era. Postcard, ca. 1899.

hot spot in England's Lake District. The hotel scored an immediate hit. By July 19 of its inaugural season, thirty guests had registered "and orders for rooms are coming in fast," claimed the newspaper that day. Not bad for a hotel that could accommodate "from 50 to 75 guests," so the paper of July 12, 1890, tells us.

As he began divesting himself of his Port Huron holdings, preparatory to moving to Chicago, in 1890 Mr. Ward and his partners sold the successful hotel to William W. Watkins, the wealthy Chicago businessman who summered at his Gratiot Beach cottage above the Windermere. Chicago folk were rare birds at Lake Huron, but Mr. Watkins had a connection to Port Huron's resorts that accounts for his building his cottage there: his brother-in-law Daniel Tilden (their wives were sisters) ran the dining hall down the shore at Huronia.

That same year, 1890, Mr. Watkins brought from Chicago to the Windermere its most famed manager, Jay O. West. Only thirty years of age at the time, Mr. West just happened to be Mr. Watkins's nephew by marriage—his wife Jennie was the daughter of Mr. Tilden of the Huronia dining hall—and furthermore he had named his son William Watkins West. The resorts were raking in money; why not let the family in on it?

Whether naming his son after the rich uncle was a bid to enter good graces we don't know, but together now in Port Huron the capable Watkins-West team set about expanding their Windermere Hotel. The following year, 1891, the place quintupled in capacity, boasting seventy-five guest rooms.

"Manager West," as the *Port Huron Daily Times* dubbed him, had talent for advertising, and the hotel quickly soared to heights of popularity among summering midwesterners during its short season of mid-June to mid-September. In 1895 Mr. West bought the place outright from his uncle, and promptly reached out to solicit business from locals, who after 1894 could ride the new electric trolley cars out to the Windermere, the last stop on the line:

> The Windermere has been extensively overhauled for the
> summer trade. Manager West will make a specialty of furnishing
> Sunday meals for Port Huron people. (June 10, 1896)

The menus for those Sunday dinners—soon just about the fanciest in Port Huron—Mr. West printed in the Saturday newspaper to tempt locals and resorters to reserve a table. Sunday, June 28, 1896, for example, enticed with oxtail soup à l'Anglais, Lake Superior white fish, boiled beef tongue with sauce Madeira, sweetbreads financière, chocolate puffs, lemon pie, and pineapple sherbet—hopefully not served all at once.

Talented businessman Mr. West kept improving his property and making sure the newspaper knew about it:

> A waiting room has been built in connection with the hotel for
> convenience of guests who patronize the electric street railway.
> (July 31, 1890)

The Winder-
mere's dining
room, around
1915. Simple yet
efficient.

The office of the Windermere has been furnished with a commo-
dious "Hurry up" filing cabinet and copying press. (August 21,
1897)

So the customers kept flocking in:

At the Windermere Mr. West is still planning to know how to
refuse the urgent applications from every direction for accommodations and a large number of people are yet waiting for
promised rooms as soon as they can be secured. (August 28,
1899)

Having come to life in 1886 and expanded in 1891, but still bursting with
guests, in 1900 the light-green Windermere grew yet again. Heralding its
success as a hostelry, twin octagonal turrets, capped by tall flagpoles, now
graced the gambrel roofline of the Windermere as an architectural flourish,
lending the simple structure a touch of grandeur and distinction. Quite the
showplace and pride of the Beaches:

The summer season at Gratiot Beach begins on Friday with the
opening of the Windermere hotel. . . . The enlargement of the
building has given a magnificent improvement in the porches
fronting on the lake, the floor space of which now aggregates

278 feet in length. . . . A minor improvement in the main hallway is the construction of a large closet for bell boys' occupancy
in which ice and water tanks are also placed. . . . A very neat improvement has been made in the sitting room on the first floor
opposite the office. . . . It will be heated when needed by either
grate and open fire or a stove. . . . (June 14, 1900)

Even with two expansions in fourteen years the Windermere could hardly
accommodate its fans. Plenty showed up without reservations.

Landlord West was forced on Friday night to adopt the time-honored cot in order to provide sleeping accommodations for a
portion of his guests. (August 11, 1900)

The Windermere is crowded and guests have been put in every
nook and corner until finally the management has been forced
to turn people away. A party arrived on Thursday evening expecting accommodations but they could not be had at the hotel

*The Windermere in summer glory, after the remodeling of
1900 extended the building and added the two turrets for a
touch of class. July 1911.*

and W. W. Watkins generously donated a portion of his spacious cottage for their occupancy. (August 8, 1903/H)

Amusingly, but not surprisingly for the famed resort,

Manager West received on Friday a letter addressed "Windermere Hotel, Windermere, Mich." (July 6, 1901)

How much did guests pay to stay at the Windermere?

The terms for the present season have been fixed at $2 per day and $10 and $11 per week. Special rates will be offered for families. (May 4, 1901)

By contrast, at the top end of the scale the posh Grand Hotel at Mackinac Island, living up to its name, charged $3 to $5 a night (equaling $21 to $35 a week) when it opened in 1887. In line with prevailing society at Gratiot and Huronia, then, the Windermere priced itself for guests of means but not for the poshest set.

What about toilets? Almost certainly Windermere bedchambers as built in 1886 did *not* boast toilets, or even sinks; indoor plumbing was still too

Something for kids, and grownups too. May 4, 1901.

THE **WINDERMERE**....

GRATIOT BEACH,
PORT HURON, MICHIGAN.

FAMILY SUMMER HOTEL.

(Twelfth season under present management)

Situated on Lake Huron, within the northern limits of the City of Port Huron.

Fine Bathing, Boating and Fishing.
Music and Dancing every evening.

Electric Light, City Water and all modern conveniences.
Electric Car from Port Huron.

RATES—$2.00 per day, and $10.00 to $14.00 per week.

Send for booklet.   Open June 15 to September 15.

J. O. WEST, Manager,
Port Huron, Mich.

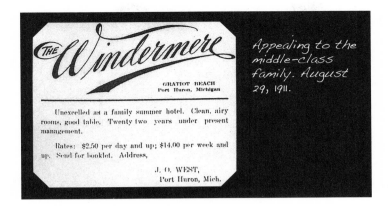

Appealing to the middle-class family. August 29, 1911.

expensive at the time, for all but the grandest hostelries.[17] Each floor might feature perhaps four "water closets" for use during the day. If you had to go during the night, most people used the chamber pots in the rooms, which the staff emptied in the morning.

Possibly the 1900 expansion did at least add sinks in the higher-end guest chambers. Otherwise, guests washed up with the pitchers and bowls provided in each room, at bath time heading down the hall to the bathing rooms on each floor, as with the toilets. Water at the Windermere came directly from the lake in the early years, as it did at Huronia, before the city installed water mains out to the beaches in 1894.

As at Huronia, entertainment at the Windermere ran a wide gamut of parties and dances. Some guests proved mighty popular:

> H. Crane, one of the season's guests at the Windermere, left
> today much to the regret of the residents of the hotel, where he
> has been the life of the party. The ladies especially are desirous
> that he may return next season in time for the races, where his
> genial presence helped them to bear their losses cheerfully.
> (August 20, 1895)

But interlopers—particularly from wannabe-rival Maple Villa, Marcus Young's hotel across the road—could expect a figurative slap on the hotel's "piazza," as porches were called back then:

> We walked over to the lake shore and took seats on the veranda
> of the Hotel Windermere. Soon a big burly, baldheaded individ-
> ual came out and asked us if we had been to dinner and when I
> told him that we had patronized Maple Villa he told us that we
> would have to get off of the piazza as he did not propose to fur-
> nish a resting or loafing place for people who took their dinner
> somewhere else. (July 25, 1900)

Early-arriving cottagers at Gratiot might find the beach pretty quiet before
the Windermere and Huronia opened each season. Opening day meant
summer was here in earnest, and with it plenty more folks with whom to
socialize.

> The hotel opened yesterday. Ruth went to Fort Gratiot yesterday
> evening and said there were several autos back of the hotel and
> in the sheds across the road. We suppose town people came out
> to supper. She saw no signs of life about Huronia, though it was
> advertised to open the 15th. (June 20, 1915/ADG)

Alongside the society names, now and again the Port Huron paper mentioned "downstairs" people—the staff who kept the hotel running. After all,
most were quite well known to hotel guests and resorters alike. Nor were
denizens of the servants' quarters totally forgotten in the summer fun:

> In Windermere hall a party will be given for the employees of
> the hotel, which consist mostly of college and high school stu-
> dents, and also the employees from Gratiot beach and Huronia
> dining hall. (August 15, 1917)

Some patrons expected employees to know their place:

> Because the waiter girls go swimming in Lake Huron at the same
> time the guests do, some of the guests have lodged a formal
> protest with the management of the Hotel Windermere.

"The lake is so large," says the manager of the hotel, "that we don't see how we can prevent the girls taking a dip in it."

Some mean things are being said about the protestors. "It's the wives of the resorters making the kick," is one story. "They're sore because the men guests show an inclination to teach the maids to float, and leave their wives to paddle around alone."

Another allegation is that "they're trying to make the girls go swimming in Black River." The "humor" in this last consists in a locally notorious condition. Even a carp, which isn't a fastidious fish, won't swim in Black River. (August 4, 1907/KG)

The clerks may have chuckled ever so slightly when

A couple of young gentlemen have thought to win a measure of notoriety at the Windermere by registering, the one as from Sing Sing prison and the other from Jackson prison. (July 24, 1895)

At the Windermere on Thursday, three Port Huron and St. Clair misses were registered as being from Havana, Santiago, and Manila [battle sites of the then-raging Spanish-American War]. (June 25, 1898)

When Mr. West died unexpectedly in April 1914, at the young age of fifty-four, the *Port Huron Times Herald* recapped his life in its front-page obituary:

Every summer for years past, Jay O. West was on hand to welcome the many people who came from other cities to spend the season at Gratiot beach or at the Windermere hotel, of which Mr. West was owner and manager.

In practically every large city in the country, Mr. West had a little circle of friends who had partaken of his hospitality during their visit in Port Huron. Much of the credit for the development of Gratiot beach is due to Mr. West . . . From a small summer hotel, with a limited number of rooms, Mr. West gradually en-

The Windermere in its glory days as the grande dame of the beach. Postcard, ca. 1910.

larged his hotel until today it is known all along the Great Lakes and in many inland cities as one of the most popular of summer places. (April 3, 1914)

Mr. West's widow sold the hotel to local businessmen, who kept it running, but the end for the venerable inn came only six years after his death, unexpectedly, when flames broke out in the west wing garret at midday on Sunday, August 29, 1920. Faulty wiring may have done it, but whatever the cause, the fire spread quickly through the old wooden barn, and when firemen finally managed to put out the flames nearly the entire building lay in a smoking heap. At least no one was injured.

The day the Windermere burned, my grandmother Agnes was penning a letter to her husband Theodore from her cottage a quarter mile north of the hotel:

The fiery demise of the Windermere, as seen from the south, August 29, 1920.

As I was sitting here writing this Mother said she smelled wood smoke. Just then Prewitt came in to say that sirens we had been hearing were fire sirens. I went out on the porch and down behind that willow break there was a dense cloud of smoke. Dinner was about ready but I dashed off for I was afraid it was down at Aunt Charlotte's. It proved to be the Windermere. When I got there people were carrying out trunks, furniture, bedding, and everything they could lay their hands on. I helped drag all sorts of things down onto the sand. I must have been there a half hour or more, then came up home. I met Mother taking our three oldest down. We had dinner, then we all went down. When I left the first time, most of the fire was confined to the dining room and back of the building. When I went back the dining room and offices were a blackened mass, the steps were burning and all the north end. Very shortly the whole north end caved in, leaving two brick chimneys standing. When we left at about 3:15 the south end of the hotel was still standing and the fire was practically out, though smoldering. I took a picture of

the building burning, then took one of the tennis court filled
high with furniture, trunks, bedding and clothes. While I was
dressing the children about four o'clock it began to rain and has
rained ever since, quite hard. We have been wondering what
became of all the household stuff on the beach.

Though the wind was so strong, fortunately "The Oaks"
[cottage adjacent to the hotel] did not catch fire. Had it caught it
would have gone hard with the other ones up this way. Everyone
near there had their hose out on their roofs. "The Oaks" was
kept wet from the start. I am enclosing a spark that I picked up
in our back yard! Think of it! Embers are scattered all along the
beach, how much farther up than our house I don't know but
you can get some idea of the breeze that was blowing. Just think
what might have happened had "The Oaks" caught. (August 29,
1920/AGB)

The unexpected demise of the old hotel along Gratiot Beach, a fixture of the
resort since its founding, touched many. That week the Beach newspaper
The Resorter ran a poignant editorial alongside its story recounting the fire:

*Hustling furniture out to the Windermere's
tennis court during the fire, August 29, 1920.*

Above: North end of the hotel during the fire. Lone survivor (left): the lobby chimney.

As the *Resorter* goes to press for this, the last issue of the 1920 season, it is with sadness that we write this final tribute to an old friend—The Windermere. It may seem strange to refer to a hotel as an old pal and friend, but when one stops to think that The Windermere was the pioneer in blazing the way for the development of the fine stretch of beach homes, it is not amiss to take the structure of wood and brick and stone and make of it a personality. For thirty-five years, during the balmy months of summer, The Windermere reflected all that is good and healthful and pleasant in life. Its halls and corridors echoed with the laughter of happy people. Within its warm and cheery embrace old age and youth have been lulled to sleep only to awaken with the morning sun as it traced its way across the lake which lay at the hotel's very door.

Generations of men and women have come and gone and treasured among the memories of their sunset days were the pleasant, happy hours they spent within the walls of The Windermere or resting on its spacious porch looking at the distant horizon and wondering what was awaiting beyond the dead line where sky and water clasped silent hands. Youth and love romped hand in hand across the stretch of sandy beach, and from the windows of The Windermere old age looked on with an approving smile.

Above left: Gratiot Inn's Florida-style Mission architecture heralded a new kind of hotel when it opened on the lake in 1917. Postcard, ca. 1920. Above right: Chinaware reflected the inn's "lakeside elegance." Right: Inviting the locals, June 19, 1938.

The people of Port Huron and its vicinity with their friends are invited to attend

THE FORMAL OPENING
AND DINNER DANCE
OF

GRATIOT INN

SIX O'CLOCK

ON THE EVENING OF JUNE 25th.

I appreciate sincerely the patronage and the encouragement received last summer from Port Huron and take this occasion to assure every one of a genuine welcome here—now and in the future.

WILLIAM ATKINSON, Manager

The Elegant Windermere

> The Windermere is no more. An old friend has passed. An old
> pal has done its bit to make the world happy and like many of
> the men and women of other years, who now know what await-
> ed them beyond the curtain, it is but ashes. (September 3, 1920)

Looking back, in a way the fiery death of the venerable inn seems symbolic, of the changing of the guard. Three years before the Windermere burned, a swank young rival had opened for business along the lake, just beyond Gratiot Beach. The cocky Gratiot Inn was everything the Windermere was not: splashy (Spanish Mission design, a rare bird in Michigan), modern (hot and cold running water and telephone in each room, private bath in most), and luxurious (cocktail lounge, even a swimming pool—heated, no less). The world of hotels had moved on. Compared to the new kid on the block, the aging dowager seemed positively, well, nineteenth century.

And so Gratiot Inn went on to blaze its own glorious path where the Windermere left off. When the elegant inn with its patio arcade fronting Lake Huron fell to the wreckers in 1969, though, the summer hotel business on southern Lake Huron, which began with the Windermere in 1886, reached the end of the line. It had lasted a scant eighty-three years.

Chapter 3
Dining In, Dining Out

It's one thing to pick a scenic spot for a resort, build the cottages, and attract the customers. It's quite another to feed them.

Huronia cottages had no kitchen, as we have seen, so the question of where to eat would surely have given potential vacationers pause in the first two seasons, when resorters were on their own for meals. That situation clearly couldn't last if the place were to thrive, so in 1882 Mr. Young opened the Huronia dining hall, which proved such a success that he enlarged it that autumn.

In 1884 newcomer Daniel Tilden, a cheesemaker in his native New York State, came to Huronia to manage the hall and promptly blossomed as the resort restaurateur. The eatery clearly raked in profits, despite being a seasonal restaurant open but ninety days or so each year, because in May 1887, only three years after his arrival, the hardworking Mr. Tilden bought the Huronia dining hall and its contents outright from Mr. Young. Selling off his resort's dining hall may seem a bit quirky, but Mr. Young was always short of cash and no doubt conceived the idea as a way to raise capital to further expand his resort.

The deed of sale painstakingly recorded every artifact that went with the hall. Among the more interesting items numbered 1 grocers' scale, 4 ice chests, 254 wooden dining chairs, 42 tables, 25 lamps, 1 dried beef cutter, 2 cherry pitters, 1 apple parer, 15 hat racks, 540 napkins, 88 tablecloths, 4 call bells, 90 pewter tablespoons, 131 pie plates, 23 pickle dishes, 170 butter chips, 31 toothpick holders, 11 three-gallon crocks, 1 rolling pin, 1 large bell in the dining hall, 2 ice tongs, 1 butter ladle, 1 bread toaster, 3 iron kettles, 6 dripping pans, 31 jelly tins, 2 ice cream freezers, 8 lanterns, 25 bread tins, 4 pancake griddles, 2 fly traps, and 5 steamers. Presumably the kitchen sink went too.

The help's quarters included 14 cots, 78 comforters, 7 bedsteads, 9 mattresses, 19 pillows, 7 looking glasses, and 6 wash boards. From the number of cots and beds we can guess that some twenty-one people served as "help" at Huronia dining hall at the time—of whom most slept on cots (presumably the lower-ranking servers). While the dining hall's table linens went into town for washing, apparently the staff did their own laundry, or perhaps that chore was assigned to a laundry maid.

The Mildred Pierce of the 1890s, Mr. Tilden opened his hall to everyone, not just resorters, and brought "Dining at Huronia" to new heights:

> Mr. Tilden, the proprietor of the dining hall at Huronia Beach, is
> meeting with the success he so richly deserves. He has 35 tables
> in the hall, seating over 200 people. (July 14, 1894)

Filled to capacity once more over the summer of 1896, Mr. Tilden extended the dining hall yet again so as to seat 300 people at newly bought tables and chairs. He certainly kept the place up to date and tidy:

> At the dining hall Manager Tilden has made a very liberal ex-
> penditure in paint, and . . . the hall is being wired today for the
> electric light. (June 19, 1896)

> Daniel Tilden claims, and with apparent correctness, that he has
> the neatest dining hall and kitchen to be found in the state. (July
> 16, 1898)

. . . and was patriotic, to boot:

> Daniel Tilden floats the Stars and Stripes above Huronia dining
> hall. (July 3, 1897)

. . . not to mention musical:

Going in to Sunday dinner at Tilden's dining hall, Huronia Beach, 1905.

The Times is in receipt of the following from the Huronia Beach dining hall [to the tune of "Columbia, the Gem of the Ocean"]:

> Huronia's the gem of Lake Huron,
> The home of the gay and the free;
> The shrine of each cottager's devotion,
> A host offers homage to thee. (September 5, 1899)

The flood of diners pouring in his doors made Mr. Tilden think outside the box. What if he built a small hotel of his own beside his dining hall, smack in the middle of Huronia, cashing in on the insatiable demand for more hotel rooms at the lake? In the ensuing legal tussle with Marcus Young, Tilden relinquished his dreams of grandeur, in return for a concession: henceforth all Huronia cottagers had to take their meals at Tilden's dining hall.

Emerging satisfied (?) from the dining hall, 1905.

By 1901, the resort was spinning the Must Eat In The Dining Hall decree as a positive advantage:

> Perhaps the most unique resort to be found anywhere is Huronia
> Beach on Lake Huron. . . . But there is one rule that cannot
> be broken. There must be no housekeeping anywhere on the
> beach. Summer resorters do not want to be bothered figuring
> out the daily menu card and here they are relieved from that
> annoyance. All the guests of Huronia eat at a central dining hall,
> a separate table for each family. . . . This has greatly added to
> the popularity of Huronia. (June 22, 1901)

Judging from newspaper accounts, the cooking ban at Huronia didn't hurt the resort's business. Even so, one wonders just how popular the "no cooking in the cottage" policy really was. It may seem a good idea at first glance, but most people might tire of regimented mealtimes and dining-hall fare, yearning for Mother's special sweet potatoes or the occasional late-night snack.

Despite serving three meals a day, dining hall waitresses still kicked up their heels after work:

> The dining room girls of Huronia dining hall have the use of
> Resort Hall for Wednesday evening and will give a dancing
> party for their friends at the Beaches and in the city. (August 28,
> 1895)

We don't know much about who worked at the hall, except that local folk could find summer jobs there. Management indulged them now and then:

> On Thursday evening the employees of the Tilden dining hall
> at Huronia beach were pleasantly surprised . . . in the shape
> of an invitation to a supper in the dining hall. Covers laid for
> twenty-five were greatly appreciated by the house staff, all of
> whom spoke of their employers in the highest terms. (September
> 5, 1903/H)

You had to register to take meals at the hall. This led to light amusement:

> Some Ohio young lady has placed the name of Gov. William
> McKinley on the Huronia register as a guest in the dining hall.
> (August 10, 1896)

> The people from St. Louis have originated a unique way of
> advertising the fair there next summer and when signing their
> name on the register at Huronia beach and other places put
> "1904" or "World's Fair" instead of St. Louis. (July 25, 1903/H)

When he fell ill in 1898, Mr. Tilden profited from the presence of a prominent big-city physician among the pioneer resort families summering at neighboring Gratiot:

> Daniel Tilden, of the Huronia dining hall, has been suffering
> from a painful illness for some days. He has been fortunate in
> having the services of Dr. Taylor, of Cincinnati, an old-time
> cottager at the beach. (September 3, 1898)

Alas, even Dr. Taylor's ministrations couldn't fix whatever ailed Mr. Tilden. When he died in Ann Arbor in November 1899, his family returned Mr. Tilden's remains to Port Huron for burial at Lakeside Cemetery, across the road from his famed summer eatery. As the season opened the next spring, Mr. Tilden received posthumous tribute in the town paper:

> The old-time patrons of the Huronia dining hall will very much
> miss the familiar face and welcome of other years, which were
> seen and heard in the person of Daniel Tilden, who was univer-
> sally respected. (June 16, 1900)

But the dining hall stayed within the family. Mr. Tilden's widow, Henrietta, took over the busy place, asking her brother Levi Fretts and his wife to come over from Chicago to help her run it. Business boomed as always:

> The Tilden dining hall at Huronia beach has been taxed to its
> utmost this summer and people have had to be turned away.
> (July 25, 1903/H)

By 1914, however, the aging Mrs. Tilden had sold the hall. Culinary standards under the new management seem to have slipped in comparison to the golden days of yore, prompting some patrons (at least, some teenagers) not only to object to the dining hall cuisine, but to thumb their noses at the prohibition against cooking in one's own cottage:

Everyone is raving because the chicken was decidedly overaged
at dinner. (July 19, 1914/JIB)

Katharine and I got so tired of the poor food at the Dining
Hall that we decided to keep house, in spite of Mr. Young. . . .
We didn't have much but sweet things for dinner, but that was
because we were just starting. We need money, too. (July 20,
1914/JIB)

The "Mr. Young" these impertinent teenagers were challenging was Marcus's
son Milo, since the old man had died the previous summer. One doubts they
would have dared challenge the venerable lion of the beach, were he still
alive. Or would have needed to, were the Tildens still in charge at Huronia
dining hall.

Chapter 4
The Beckoning Lake

So now that your journey from home was done, you'd settled in your cottage, signed up for meals or done your grocery shopping (depending on your accommodations), and were ready to cavort in the big, beautiful lake that had lured you there in the first place. How might you amuse yourself in its welcoming, salt-free waters? For starters, surely everyone was going swimming, that invigorating recreation—and great leveler of the social classes.

> FOR THE WATER NYMPHS
>
> The time of year has arrived when every little piece of water big enough to get into assumes an inviting glassiness of surface and warm limpidity of depth that tempt one to plunge in regardless of consequences. . . . At any rate, it is a very innocent pleasure and a very leveling one. . . . The wet hair of the mistress and of the maid looks equally like seaweed, and the nose of the patrician and of the proletariat burns regardless of class distinctions. (August 15, 1894)

By 1897 both resorts and the Windermere boasted diving platforms and springboards in the lake, which encouraged ingenuity:

> A recent invention at the diving platform at Gratiot is a slanting board from the top of the platform. It is covered with copper and kept bright with various sliding processes. (August 21, 1897)

All those resorters in the water presented an opportunity for remuneration:

> Some competent gentleman can find a large class of young people anxious to take swimming lessons at both the beaches. (July 26, 1897)

Although some turned their noses up at actually going *into* the lake:

> A gentleman from the city who is spending a few days at Gratiot,
> forsakes Lake Huron with all the dignity of a judge and comes
> downtown for a bath in his own tub. (August 21, 1897)

While others got a rub when they *did* go in the lake:

A TIDAL WAVE
Several People at Holland Beach Came Near Drowning
> On Sunday the water rose nearly two feet at Holland beach and
> E. J. Schoolcraft, Ed Campbell and Frank Philbrick came near
> being swept out into the lake. An investigation revealed the
> cause of this sudden tidal wave. It seems that Burt Duffie was out
> rowing in a boat at Keewahdin beach and fell overboard. (July
> 25, 1899)

NO SEA SERPENT.
False Report Circulated Regarding City Clerk Wagenseil
> The report around the city hall that Wm. F. Wagenseil discovered
> a sea serpent off Keewahdin park early Friday morning is untrue.
> He found on investigation that John B. McIlwain was in bathing.
> (July 20, 1907)

Some people thought of new ways to splash around:

> The throng of bathers . . . was organized into a dancing party in
> the water on Thursday morning and several figures of a quadrille
> were carried out. The idea created a large amount of sport. It
> originated with Mrs. T. A. Goulden. (August 11, 1900)

One "professor" revived a celebrated biblical episode:

> The exhibitions of W. C. Soule, who was announced to walk on
> the water at Huronia Beach on Tuesday, proved a failure. Mr.

Agnes Greene, Theodore Brookes, Clark Greene (Agnes's brother), Mr. Engle, Bert Riggs (Ada's cousin, son of Rev. Riggs of the Beach Chapel), Ada Greene, Nellie Dunlap, and Howard Dunlap (Ada's brother).

Soule found his "walk-in-the-water" shoes rather unreliable and was obliged to call in assistance to prevent him from drowning. Quite a number of people from this city and Fort Gratiot were attracted to the spot by his announcements. (July 10, 1890)

Prof. W. C. Soule, who gave an exhibition of walking on water at Huronia Beach Tuesday last, was a caller at The Times office today. He denies that he came near drowning. He says it is a part of his programme to fall into the water. The audience were of the opinion that the entertainment was a fizzle, but the above explanation will probably remove the wrong impression. Mr. Soule thinks he has a valuable patent. (July 11, 1890)

You didn't need fancy water toys to savor the lake:

We had a lot of fun in bathing with a big, smooth log, rolling and riding on it. (August 6, 1914/JIB)

Dear Bobbie, I am waiting to hear that you have ducked all of
your head under water at once. When you do so, please let me
know about it. (August 16, 1921/TPB)

Tell the children not to splash me in effigy. (July 30, 1922/JIB)

Something about Lake Huron stones and shells has always inspired gath-
erers:

We picked up the curious and interesting pebbles which line the
beach, venturing rashly after those deceptive ones so brilliant in
the water, so dull when dry. (August 15, 1882/MF)

How about fishing right from the beach, or in a fishing party:

There is splendid fishing in the lake, and large catches of both
perch and pickerel are being made all along the beaches. (June
27, 1896)

Messrs. Tennant, Chapman, McChesney and Miller, cottagers at
Huronia, chartered a tug last week to Kettle Point for a fishing
trip. They caught 143 bass and a 15-pound muskellunge. They
had the fish served for two days at the dining hall. The party
won a host of compliments from the other cottagers for their
generosity. (July 7, 1900)

If you didn't care for a dip, you could row or sail on the lake, if you had a
boat.

Lake Huron . . . is coming to be known as a most delightful
boating resort for downtown people. Said an enthusiastic young
lady after an hour's row on the lake, "This just beats a wheel!"
(July 11, 1896; a "wheel" being a bicycle)

Elsie Riggs of Cincinnati demonstrating proper Gratiot Beach boating attire, 1902.

If you were lucky enough to finagle one of the newfangled outboard motors that began appearing around 1907, you could impress the folks on the beach with your speed—provided you could get the thing started:

> Grandmother Greene bought us a new 14-h.p. Evinrude
> outboard. It weighed about a hundred pounds and had to be
> started by winding the rope around the flywheel and yanking
> it — no battery-operated starters then. You had to pull the rope
> smartly to get the job done, something for which our tender
> frames were not optimal. Besides, after the machine had lain

around all winter, things happened to it — like bumblebees setting up housekeeping inside.

Yanking the rope could be pretty frustrating. My brother Prewitt and I would each give several yanks, then throw down the rope frustrated, and let the other try.

Either way you took a lot of punishment. The yanker got a sore arm trying, but like as not the other fellow got a whipping across the back since the rope lashed out behind the puller. So the puller had to catch the rope in the left hand to subdue it and spare the passengers.

To help matters we devised a way to tilt the motor up so you didn't have to overcome the resistance of the water in this clutch-less contraption. Once the motor caught, firing happily, you tried to let it gently down into the water so you could take off. Still it would slam against the transom, and there was a fair chance that you, standing in the boat, would be sat down unceremoniously as the craft took off. (RDB Huronia)

Prewitt Brookes in his speedboat, 1929.

Clark brought us home in the motorboat. There were seven of
us, and the boat sides were only two inches from the water. Our
balance was delicate. (July 23, 1914/JIB)

Harnessed Clark's 35-mosquito-power motor to the grandsire of
boats and took Julia, Jean, and Louise for a trip up Black River
yesterday evening. The trip was uneventful though it did result
in a pillow fight between Julia and Louise when they returned.
Jean tried to make them be good by licking them both but suffered the usual fate of the peacemaker. (July 17, 1916/TPB)

Understand you have a motorboat with which I suppose you are
having much pleasure. Save a ride for me, will you? Belonging
to the "Safety First" club, I will ask that you have the motor in
good order—plenty of gasoline & oil—all leaks caulked—and
last but not least a pair of good oars each secured to its own
lock by chain or stout rope to prevent danger in case motor
stalls—also an SOS signal whistle for distress—Suppose of course
you will give the boat a good coat of paint for the winter & the
disconnected engine a thorough cleansing & oilings—so as to be
in good condition for 1928. (August 27, 1927/HSB)

Since Huronia resorters were renters, they wouldn't have their own boat, so
the resort accommodated them.

Baldwin & Dickman have erected a large tent on the beach at
the north end of Huronia and have a half-dozen boats ready for
business. They will put up another tent for bathers. (June 23,
1900)

Starting in the 1920s, you might water-ski if you had a boat with an engine
big enough to pull skiers out of the water. When my father bought our
speedboat, in 1958, Gratiot Inn became the accepted limit of the typical

water-ski run, involving a graceful loop in the blue waters off the inn, to head back to the cottage. Unless, that is, the sibling driving the boat were feeling devilish, in which case a sharp hairpin turn ("cracking the whip") sent the skier hurtling outside the boat's wake and, at least in my case, ignominious dunking in icy Lake Huron, as the inn guests watched serenely from their lounge chairs under its Spanish-looking arcade. Unwittingly, they were just part of the time-honored tradition of entertaining yourself, if you didn't have a boat, by watching the travails of those who did.

The capsizing of a sailing yacht near the lightship on Tuesday gave the men on the dredge and people at the beaches a ripple of excitement. Fortunately the young man on the yacht was saved from drowning. (August 8, 1896)

A small steam yacht ran into the shelter of Keewahdin Beach Wednesday morning and sent three sea-sick passengers ashore, one at a time. . . . At the above point the ladies became so disenchanted with the beautiful waters of Lake Huron that they

Spin on Lake Huron, Gratiot Beach, 1930.

decided they would prefer to continue their journey overland.
(August 31, 1900)

Four young ladies were overturned in a sailboat yesterday afternoon opposite Gratiot beach. . . . The young ladies were rescued
without much difficulty and a thorough soaking and a bad scare
were the only results of the accident. (August 9, 1902/H)

Lake Huron is known for its sudden fury:

A violent squall of short duration came down the lake Sunday
afternoon at about 4:20 and several young people around
the beaches and further up the lake had narrow escapes from
drowning.
  The *Emma B* capsized about a mile above the Windermere
and James and Dan McDonald, two young men who were on
the yacht, spent a half hour in the water clinging to the boat.
They were finally taken off by two boys who went out in a row-
boat from the Windermere. (August 19, 1895)

Lake Huron was in one of her wildest moods on Thursday, and
grate fires were popular in the afternoon in the cottages. (July
22, 1898)

The U.S. Life-Saving Service, forerunner of the Coast Guard, wanted you to
know they were ready to haul you out of the lake if need be:

There were a couple of hundred . . . resorters gathered on the
beach where the life saving crew gave an exhibition drill. The
feat of overturning the life boat and coming up again on the
inside when it turned upright again was done many times to the
wonder of those who had not seen it done before and to the
admiration of all. When the exhibition was over and the crew

rowed to shore . . . the onlookers gave them hearty applause
and paid them fine compliments. (August 15, 1903)

Until waterside resorts came into being as summer destinations, no one in
their right mind spent much time on a beach. By the 1890s, though, roast-
ing oneself on the sunny shore was the rage, sparking a bemused reaction
in some:

> The rush to the beaches increases every year, and as things look
> now, in another few seasons half our population will spend the
> summer on the shore. It is amusing to see a person who can't
> endure the heat in a cool and airy house in town, get on a bicy-
> cle and ride ever so many miles in the blazing sunshine to the
> lakeshore and then bake himself in the hot sand to get cooled
> off. The power of imagination is a wonderful thing! (August 11,
> 1898)

You might bake yourself on the beach, but swimsuits of the day kept you
pretty fully clothed. Exposing your hide itself to the sun at the beach—sun-
bathing—became the thing to do only in the 1920s, when fashion launched
its assault on prewar modesty, allowing swimsuits to reveal more skin. It also
raised eyebrows, among the older generation; septuagenarian Ada Greene's
letter of August 30, 1922, berated the local beach newspaper for its "pictures, little but bathers in the extreme style of modern suits I blush to see."
Twenty years later, swimsuits were skimpier still:

> SUMMER RESORT:—a place where each girl says she has nothing
> to wear and, I say, she wears it. (August 9, 1942/TPB)

Modesty in revealing flesh aside, the Victorian years distinguished a lady
by how porcelain-like her skin was, not how bronzed. Once people took to
sunning their carcass on the beach and in the water, however, no sunscreen
existed to keep that complexion porcelain, since sun lotion wasn't invented
until World War II:

Chic Little Bathing Frock.

BATHING STYLES AT THE BEACHES THIS SEASON.

Dive Right Into This

Wool Bathing Suit Bargain at $3.00

How much nicer it feels to swim in an all wool bathing suit; how much nicer it looks when you step up on the beach.

Above left: Chic maybe, but not so little, and leaving much to the imagination. August 27, 1900. Above right: The hemline and sleeves had risen a bit by May 31, 1902. Below: Gentleman's attire ca. 1925. Who wouldn't want to wear wool to the beach?

Theodore came down with his amateur motorboat to take some-body into town via Black River, so we yelled for Miss O'Hooligan, and hitched our waterwagon on his. I, with a wisdom

Bathing poseurs, Gratiot Beach, 1908.

beyond my years, put on a coat and a hat, and kept my hands
covered up, but Lib and Katharine and Miss O'Ferrall let the sun
come right through their waists [blouses]. And you ought to see
the color they've been all week—Harry's ox-blood shoes are
about the same shade. They've made the nights hideous with
their lamentations. (July 9, 1916/JIB)

Going to the beach constituted an act of courage—you were exposing your
hide and your fashion sense to the judgment of your fellow beachers:

If I had a trick sun suit like Peg's I'd be down on the beach with
my wife as she reads the Sunday School papers. If I just had a
figure maybe I'd go down in my old nondescript. Believe I shall
just go anyhow. Cheerio!! (September 3, 1944/TPB)

If you weren't on the beach or in the lake, you could simply plunk down
in the rocking chair on the porch and soak up the view. After all, this was
the heyday of Great Lakes shipping. Whereas nowadays it's jaw-dropping if
fifteen ships steam by on a summer's day, we know from the paper that fully

184 vessels sailed past the Beaches on July 12, 1896, and 160 on July 4, 1897 (the record days for both those years, says the *Daily Times* of September 2, 1897).

> More than once I have looked up and down the water and have said, "There, for the first time, not a vessel in view!" No, not so fast! There is a topmast looming up and there is the smoke of a steamer. This procession is so continuous that at night one can hardly resist the impression that yonder is a city street with its illuminating lamps. They are only the lights on masts and amidship that are slowly passing along. (New York Evangelist, October 25, 1900)

> There's one of the Canadian passenger boats going by now. They furnish a variety from the ordinary run of big ore and freight and lumber steamers. These boats pass about a mile and a half from shore and it takes their swells fully fifteen minutes to reach the shore. (circa 1905/TPB)

Private sailing yachts and work boats enlivened the scene of passing commerce:

> The Messrs. Lindenberg have their sailing yacht anchored in front of the Windermere. . . . The yacht is the Defender of the beaches. (July 17, 1895)

> The musical voices from the dredges in front of the beaches on the Corsica shoals are being heard again this season. (June 19, 1896)

> The tow barge W. R. Moore created a good deal of interest all along the beaches on Friday afternoon. She was coming down the lake and became waterlogged. When she dropped her

anchors only her deck load was above water. A couple of tugs towed her to the river. (August 12, 1899)

The steam barge *Tom Adams*, held on the Corsica shoals on Friday by an accident to her machinery, was closely watched by beach residents as being a curiosity to the majority of cottagers in these days of hurrying navigation. (September 2, 1899)

Frank Fletcher's steam yacht *Winyah* from Alpena anchored in front of the Windermere on Friday evening. Her fine searchlight was seen to good advantage during the evening by Gratiot cottagers. (July 7, 1900)

The rare sight of a schooner with all canvas set sailing out of the river was seen at the beaches on Friday evening. (June 29, 1901)

Some people sailed *over* the lake, not on it:

Prof. Hamilton steered his airship along in front of Gratiot beach in his flight Thursday afternoon and gave an aerial exhibition in front of the Windermere. (July 20, 1907)

The days of sailing ships came to an end, of course, replaced by coal- and oil-fired steamers:

Right now I can see a tug pulling an old three-masted schooner down the lake. We don't see sailing boats anymore except when there are yacht races. (July 31, 1927/RDB)

With the proliferation of cars, you could quickly hie yourself down to the narrows where Lake Huron empties into the St. Clair River. Here the ships passed by so closely that you could wave to them:

Yesterday evening John and Hugh persuaded the household to journey to the riverside just north of the International Bridge. There for an hour we saw the passing freighters at close range until the D&C passenger steamer hove in sight, en route from Detroit to Duluth. Mr. and Mrs. Atkins were on deck at the rail, waving a pillow case and manipulating a pair of field glasses to observe the wildly waving arms and jumping legs on shore. They are on the way to Canada. (July 31, 1945/TPB)

It was fun to watch the ships and boats, unless the morning started out foggy:

The *North West* and a number of other boats were anchored off the beaches for several hours this morning because of the fog, and the sound of their whistles made life miserable for the cottagers. (September 5, 1895)

On April 29, 1907, the small passenger steamer *Pilgrim* ran aground off Huronia Beach, providing entertainment for the resorters that summer:

The hull is used as a diving and swimming headquarters for bathers. Someone set the wreck afire the evening of the Fourth, but it died out before anything noticeable was burned. (July 6, 1907)

The beach might not be at its best, if one of the log rafts that plied the Great Lakes in those days ran into trouble:

Raftsmen have finished gathering up the logs which washed ashore during the storm some time ago. The logs were piled two and three deep by the rough seas. (July 15, 1905)

Beeee-oooooooooooooooohhh

Steamers and sailboats came and went, but from 1893 onward the Huron Lightship formed the one constant sight in the lake for every beacher contemplating the Lake Huron horizons. It was the one vessel just about every cottager and hotel guest could identify.

Anchored originally a mile off Gratiot Beach during the busy shipping season, the lightship marked Corsica Shoals in lower Lake Huron, the shelf of shallow waters that formed a hazard to ships. At night her light warned vessels away from the shoals, directing them instead toward the dredged ship channel that led down to the St. Clair River at the foot of the lake. Resorters could easily see the little ship at anchor out in the lake, to the north, as the freighters sailed past. Over the decades at least three different lightships performed this duty at Corsica Shoals; in later years the vessel's hull sported the bold white letters H-U-R-O-N, though you needed binoculars to read them.

By the time I came on the scene, in the 1950s, the lightship took up station out on the lake in early spring, long before resort season began, having spent the winters tied up in town. But in earlier decades cottagers looked for the arrival of the little vessel in the lake to herald the true beginning of summer.

> Lightship was brought out today by a vessel & anchored for the summer; the buoy which was in its place, was taken in. (May 15, 1911/ADGdiary)

At night the big lens atop her mast sent its light around the horizons, slowly, silently, reassuringly. I could watch the gently pulsing light at night from my bed in the cottage.

When fog blanketed the lake—typically on June mornings—the lightship's steam whistle sounded its sonorous *beeee-oooooooooooooooohhh*. For resorters those two deep notes seemed somehow comforting, but the blast must have nearly split the eardrums of the men on board. To these bass

*The original Lake Huron lightship, anchored off Huronia
Beach in 1903.*

notes from the lightship each steamer added its own three whistle blasts, the
standard warning then to other vessels in fog, creating a veritable symphony
of steam out on the lake from ships you could hear but couldn't see. When
you woke up to that concert, you knew without opening your eyes that fog
had settled in.

> The fog horns moaned dolefully most of yesterday until a heavy
> rain disintegrated the fog. (September 5, 1943/TPB)

On stormy nights cottagers could give thanks for their snug beds on land,
rather than tossing about on that tiny platform in the crashing waves and
howling wind. But apart from storms, life must have seemed rather monot-
onous for the crew, stuck as they were on the lightship for thirty-day tours
of duty on board.

If you had a boat you could visit the lightship on station, with the idea
of relieving a bit of the crew's tedium while giving yourself something novel

Agnes Greene visiting the wooden lightship in 1902. In the background, the dredge deepens Lake Huron's Corsica Shoals.

to do. Teenagers in earlier years, including my father and his brother Prewitt, rowed out to her now and again, carrying magazines and books for the sailors. In later years, after around 1930, the lightship moved a couple of miles farther up the lake, which put it out of reach of rowers, but motorboats could still visit. We did in the 1950s, zooming out to the lightship maybe once a summer, puttering around it in a circle, marveling at the great black chain that anchored its bow to the bottom of the lake, waving to the Coast Guard sailors on board. Who knows what they thought of us, but they seemed friendly and waved back. They probably didn't mind the diversion.

When the last of the Huron lightships sailed off its station for the final time in 1970, replaced by an automated tower in the lake, the Beaches lost their steadfast and beloved beacon of summer.

Chapter 5
Lolling, Frolicking, Mingling

Swimming and boating, or watching those who were, of course provided the number one diversion at these waterside resorts, but how else might you spend your days, and nights?

As paying customers, surely renters at Huronia would expect management to provide them a variety of things to do besides just playing in the lake. Not so, though, in early years, when management left the clientele pretty well to their own devices for entertainment, as though providing the cottages and the view had been enough. But if resorters organized their own evening entertainments, management was happy to let them use the dining hall, cleared of tables after supper.

Nearly three hundred resorters packed the hall for the first of these events that we know about, on Saturday evening, July 17, 1886, for the "very pleasant entertainment given by the young ladies and gentlemen sojourning at 'Huronia' and 'Gratiot,'" who provided piano solos and duets, recitations, and a song by three whippersnappers calling themselves the Huronia Trio.[18] As highlight of the evening, seventeen-year-old Miss Mary Dean of Cincinnati brought down the house with her poem, "The Beach A B C's" (see chapter 10).

The next week's impromptu offering sought to maintain that high standard:

Huronia Beach Pastimes.
Saturday evening was a gala evening at Huronia Beach, Marcus Young's pleasant summer resort. The occasion was an entertainment given by the young folks of the Beach. The exercises consisted of recitations in elocution and piano-forte, and a few selections on the banjo by the genial and popular Wilson

Doty. . . . In the closing some mention was made of Mr. Young:
"Y is for Young, Marcus is his name," and Mr. Clough, of Detroit,
provoked great merriment by rising and saying—

   "Y is for Young, Marcus is his name,

   He isn't very large, but he gets there just the same." (July 26,
1886/SC)

Two years later, entertainment at Huronia was still rather tame. Since nothing much was happening at the beach, you'd head into town for a little diversion:

A party of young ladies and gentlemen from Huronia Beach
drove through the streets of the city on Thursday afternoon,
riding on an old lumber wagon drawn by Marcus Young's mules.
(July 27, 1888)

A large number of Huronia beach cottagers attended the minstrel show last night. (August 21, 1888)

Clearly this laissez-faire approach with lame amenities couldn't last. As vacationers grew accustomed to the idea of summering at resorts, they demanded more in the way of activities, and any resort that failed to indulge them risked losing customers to the vastly expanding array of holiday spots now popping up around the country. And so by the end of Huronia's first decade, Mr. Young finally coughed up the money to enhance the merrymaking offerings by building the first of several amenities that would keep his customers amused.

A dancing hall . . . a bowling alley . . . and a billiard parlor . . .
are being built at Huronia Beach. The coming season at this
pleasant resort will be the most brilliant in the history of the
beach. (April 24, 1889; never mind that the "history of the
beach" stretched back a grand total of nine years)

As Huronia grew, entertainment offerings expanded into a rich panoply of potential divertissements. Management stepped in to help organize your day almost as soon as the sun peeked over the Canadian shore, as the dining hall's "rising bell" rang out at 7:00 a.m., as of 1895, followed by the breakfast bell at 7:30. No sleeping in, even on vacation, unless you didn't mind missing breakfast. Get up and enjoy yourself, was the rule.

Having learned its lesson about providing diversions, management hired an official entertainer, as she was called. Longest-lived incumbent in the post, Mrs. Hattie Dean of Toledo (no relation to the teenage poet mentioned above), took up her duties in 1904 and quickly found her niche as the Perle Mesta of the Beach.

> Mrs. Dean, who has proved so successful for the past several years, has again taken up the work of entertaining for Huronia beach. . . . Mrs. Dean began a dancing school for the beach children Friday morning at the dance hall. (July 6, 1907)

> Mrs. Dean has the knack of keeping things moving and this summer will see many new feature entertainments. . . . The first meeting of the weekly bridge and five hundred parties will be held Friday morning in Huronia hall at 9:45 o'clock. (July 7, 1916)

Having availed yourself of Mrs. Dean's morning classes after breakfast, you might start your day with a jaunt along the sidewalk. For most everyone, strolling the sidewalk or the beach constituted not only exercise but also a major social event, in which one paid calls on neighbors and friends. The more adventuresome might try a spin on a bicycle—the national rage in the 1890s, to which Lake Huron's resorts proved no exception, for those with the energy.

> Bowers & Co. have a branch shop for bicycle repairs at the Windermere. (July 2, 1898)

Huronia patriots on tricycle: Ruth Brookes, Charles Galt, and Bobby and Prewitt Brookes, July 4, 1917.

The new fad had its drawbacks:

> The bicycle scorcher makes quite often a first-class nuisance of himself on the walk on Gratiot avenue. There certainly ought to be no necessity of ladies or children jumping into the ditch or climbing a bank to get out of the way, as has been the case too frequently of late. (September 4, 1899)

Others sought a less exhausting activity:

> In Huronia beach hall a crochet party was held Tuesday afternoon from 2:30 to 5 o'clock. (July 29, 1915)

Maybe you owned one of the new lightweight and hence portable cameras. They made photography a common hobby after 1895 or so, especially among the women travelers that Kodak's advertising targeted.[19]

Young ladies and their Kodak camera, Huronia. Beach, 1908.

Friday was an ideal day at the beaches for the kodak fiend. (August 23, 1902/H)

The Camera girls at Huronia were out in force along the shore and in small boats on the lake on Thursday afternoon. (August 15, 1903)

How about a view of Lake Huron from on high?

> The last balloon ascension of the season at Huronia beach will
> take place at the pavillion this evening. (September 5, 1895)

The game of tennis swept the country from England in the 1880s, and in the 1890s Huronia and the Windermere announced construction of "lawn tennis courts" for this game that both men and women could play. Huronia's new court was cause for revelry.

Huronia tennis champs of 1904, Milo Young and Theodore Brookes.

Agnes Greene taking on the tennis court, 1907.

There will be a grand display of fireworks at Huronia Beach
Friday night to celebrate the opening of the new tennis court.
(August 13, 1895).

The courts proved hugely popular with the summer crowd:

The tennis court at Huronia has been assigned to the use of the
adults during forenoons and the children in the afternoons. (July
22, 1899)

Gratiot Defeated.
In a contest on the Windermere tennis court Friday morning the
Gratiot beach team met defeat when the Huronia team took 3
out of 5 sets. (August 13, 1904)

Up North

Winners of tennis tournaments were properly feted:

> Harry received his tennis cup yesterday. He really responded
> very nicely to Mrs. Armstrong's presentation speech. Julia could
> not go to the tea, and Mrs. Mudd did not want Harry to do
> so, but a tea for the cup winner without that individual being
> present was not to be thought of. So I told him he had to go.
> (August 17, 1913/MPB)

But you didn't really need a court:

> Harry and Clark Greene have found a new way to play tennis.
> One stands in front of the cottage, one in the back, and they bat
> the ball over. (July 9, 1906/MPB)

For young men, the national pastime of baseball pitted the Huronia team
against any club bold enough to take them on.

> The Huronia Beach baseball club would like to play any Port
> Huron club of boys from 12 to 16 years of age. All games to be
> played on the Huronia grounds. (August 18, 1886)

Big news, when young ladies took to the baseball diamond. Wonder what
they wore:

> A revolution in Port Huron baseballdom took place at the
> diamond at Huronia beach yesterday, when a baseball nine com-
> posed of a number of young ladies who are spending the sum-
> mer at Gratiot beach played and defeated a team composed of a
> bunch of girls who are cottaging at Huronia. . . . When a young
> sunburned damsel would smash out a liner to the infield, it
> was interesting to watch her try to beat the ball to first. In most
> instances perhaps a bundle of curls would drop from behind a
> natty little cap, but nothing daunted the fair runner. . . .
> (August 10, 1910)

You thought basketball was just a guy thing in 1903?

> A feature of the entertainment at Gratiot beach is outdoor bas-
> ketball. . . . The young ladies are the most enthusiastic players.
> (August 1, 1903/H)

Care to knock down those little ten pins? Huronia had an alley, but you could also get a bowling party together to head downtown, via streetcar. It was another sport both sexes could enjoy in each others' company.

> A company of Huronia people made the second bowling party
> of the season at the Metropole alley on Lapeer avenue, on
> Friday. Upwards of 30 ladies and gentlemen were in the party.
> (August 25, 1900)

Horseback riding might divert you. But women's liberation? Not yet:

> Oh dear! No riding today. I wish Theodore would come home—
> he could probably take us out with him. Mother won't let us try
> it for the first time without a man. (July 30, 1914/JIB)

Athletics got highly organized in 1908:

> About 60 young people of Huronia beach attended a meeting
> Friday afternoon and organized the Huronia Beach Athletic as-
> sociation. Its objects are two-fold: First, to promote athletics, and
> secondly social. (July 11, 1908)

The Woman's Christian Temperance Union was on hand from the beginning, to ensure high moral standards along the shores of Lake Huron.

> The W.C.T.U. held a basket picnic at the Beach, at the cottage of
> Mrs. Henry Howard on Thursday, Aug. 19th. A large number of
> ladies were present. . . . The earnest words spoken on both sides
> will live in the memory of all who were fortunate enough to

hear them. Refreshments were served on the grounds and were
second only to the "feast of reason and flow of soul." (August
21, 1886; one presumes the refreshments were lemonade)

Some shindigs went for a good cause:

Mrs. Davidson held a cake and kimono sale at her cottage at
Gratiot this afternoon. The proceeds from the sale will go to the
organ guild of Grace church. (July 19, 1902/H)

No booze might be served at Huronia, but that didn't stop a little raciness:

Aikman Bros. have opened a racing track in the grove at Huronia, and a half dozen of their ponies are on duty there. (July 3,
1896)

Card parties attracted those who did not consider them the work of the devil.

A pleasant progressive euchre party was given at the Windermere on Thursday evening. (July 25, 1896)

Mrs. Mudd, cottage 13½, entertained a bridge Friday afternoon, followed by luncheon. (July 11, 1914)

Resorters with aspirations to presage Elsa Maxwell, and who had rented
cottages large enough, could host elaborate card soirees:

HURONIA BEACH.
One of the most enjoyable events of the season at this resort
was the progressive euchre party given on Monday evening by
Mrs. Ray, of St. Louis. . . . The favors were little ornaments of
every imaginable description, and in addition to keeping the
score in the usual manner, the very pleasant feature was introduced of keeping it on a large blackboard in the presence of
the entire company. We will make no attempt at a description

of the toilets of the ladies, suffice it to say, they were elegant. The cottage was well lighted and beautifully decorated. (August 18, 1892)

Card parties could serve a good cause, too:

The fourth annual mid-summer card party given for the benefit of the Hospital Aid society was held at the Windermere dance hall Thursday afternoon. . . . The beach people . . . made donations of cooking, fancy articles and liberal sums of money to the hostesses. (August 5, 1911)

Some afternoon get-togethers took a more uplifting bent:

A musicale was given in the Huronia beach resort hall on Friday afternoon by some of the talented cottagers. . . . There are some unusually good musicians among cottagers at Huronia and they gave an appreciable concert. (August 8, 1903/H)

While other performers couldn't get the audience they deserved:

Plays Mouth Organ.
A tramp who calls himself a professor of mouth organ melody, visited the Windermere Friday afternoon. He told the clerk he walked from one resort to another, giving recitals of his mouth organ music. . . . He could not get an enthusiastic gathering around him at the Gratiot beach hotel so he continued his trip north on foot, expecting to make his way to Petoskey and other northern resorts. People who saw him at the hotel say he appears to be unbalanced. (June 25, 1904)

Maybe you wanted to escape for a bit. You could join a group outing by ship. . . .

The Star Line steamers will give a special excursion for beach people to Detroit and return on Wednesday, July 28. (July 26, 1897)

Canada, just across the lake, beckoned with the novel notion of visiting a foreign country while still in sight of home. You could take the ferry steamers from Port Huron for the short ride across the river to Sarnia, Ontario, or drive over the Blue Water Bridge after it opened in 1938:

> Yesterday evening we drove across the "Blue Water Bridge" into Canada. . . . There was nothing much to see on the roads in Canada but the drive over the bridge is beautiful and awe inspiring. (August 20, 1944/AGB)

Who knows what it looked like, but for the kiddies—

> Edward Stone's merry-go-round is receiving a liberal patronage from the younger residents at the Beaches. (August 13, 1895)

To keep those kids distracted:

Keeping the kids distracted with scooters. Ada Greene's cottage, Gratiot, 1920.

Huronia baby parade, 1912.

A Baby Parade.

Miss Claire Gordon has conceived a new entertainment for the Huronia beachers and this time it is a "baby parade." All the youngsters from three months old to five years will be in line. The smallest tots will be pushed in their go-carts. Then there will be judges to decide upon the prize baby. (August 13, 1904)

Ella sent up word for us to come down as she was going to give a Punch and Judy show for the children. Foolishly, I went too. . . . (August 20, 1920/AGB)

Marcus Young's son Huronia and his patriotic tricycle with the "Huronia" banner lead the baby parade of 1905.

Teenagers looked forward to seeing their pals again each summer, and invented their own entertainments in each other's company.

> We're expecting our friends Helen Rutledge and Adele Bonsack
> this week. There is certainly a large number of young people
> here, sixty belong to our young peoples' club and there are a
> few more besides. (July 12, 1906/TPB)

Teenage antics, Gratiot 1908: Clark Greene of Salem, Ohio, and " baby" Polly Bissell of Toledo.

We had a waist parade this evening, all of us in white skirts, and waists of all colors of the rainbow. (June 23, 1914/JIB; a "waist" being a blouse)

A sewing bee this afternoon, with refreshments of lemonade and nabiscos. (June 24, 1914/JIB)

Digging in the sand, Junior might make a startling discovery:

Thursday forenoon Master Robert Johnson, of St. Louis, Mo., came rushing into the Windermere Hotel, having in his hand something which had the appearance of a petrified potato. . . . An examination of the object showed that it was to all appearances a tooth from some species of animal long since extinct. . . .

> Master Johnson will preserve the relic until he returns to his South-
> ern home. (August 5, 1892)

And if the kiddies or their parents felt the urge for that special summer treat,

> The Mascotte ice cream rooms are again in commission at Huro-
> nia. (July 11, 1896)

Some kids did more than the time-honored goofing off all summer:

> Six children from Gratiot beach, on their own initiative, sold
> flowers and other articles during the week until they had earned
> $4.16, with which they went to a store and purchased things to
> eat for the children of the crippled camp at Edison Park beach.
> (September 5, 1919)

Huronia cottages were so close together, playgrounds could extend next
door.

> Louise is furnishing amusement to the neighbors. She has got
> all the chairs she can lay hands on in the porch in orderly rows.
> Then stepping over the Prather's railing and facing the chairs,
> proceeds to preach. Theodore expected to be ousted when he
> sat in one of the chairs, but she was well satisfied to have an
> audience. (July 12, 1908/MPB)

Maybe it *was* a simpler age, in some respects:

> Friday afternoon a unique contest was held at Resort hall, the
> object of which was to see who could draw, blindfolded, the
> best-looking horse. As a result, a large number of marks resembling
> Egyptian hieroglyphics were found on the chart. (July 15, 1905)

You would of course want summer reading while adorning the hammock
on the porch.

Louise Brookes and kittens, Huronia hammock, 1907.

A circulating library for the benefit of the Dean Memorial Chapel
has been established at Langholm Lodge at Gratiot. The mem-
bership fee is one book and the rate five cents per volume. (July
16, 1898)

Enterprising merchants and local residents produced knick-knacks to remind
you of summer at the Beaches.

O'Neill Bros. & Co. have placed a case of souvenir china of very
beautiful patterns on sale at the Windermere office. (July 26,
1897)

For resorters of all ages, the age-old sport of gossiping had its adherents, of
course:

The hammock over the sandy "lawn" at Huronia was comfy, if you didn't mind lounging in full view of the neighbors. Sisters Julia (right) and Louise Brookes of St. Louis, 1906.

Heard on two separate porches at Huronia: "It is just wonderful that any woman should be willing to marry without having a knowledge of cooking and housekeeping." And on the other: "Well, I feel a hearty sympathy for her husband." And yet neither conversation had any relation whatever to the other, nor were they heard by the participants. (September 4, 1899)

Huronia had its own post office, since the well-bred resorter considered letter writing a social duty. Besides, quite a few families had left Dad back home, and he expected regular news from the brood. That meant writing letters—lots of them. Or better yet, sending picture postcards, the new fad that swept the world in the 1890s.

> E. J. Smiley, the postmaster at Huronia beach, said to a Times
> reporter on Thursday, "Few people have any idea of the amount
> of mail matter handled during the season at the beach. . . . We
> receive mails at 7 o'clock a.m., 12 noon, 3 p.m., and 7 p.m."
> (August 5, 1892)

In 1898 Marcus Young's son Milo, in an apparent bit of nepotism, became postmaster at Huronia. The office remodeling of 1899 gave him swell digs to work in:

> The post office is the neatest to be had in furnishings and the
> best that has ever been seen at Huronia. A large number of pri-
> vate boxes are provided in addition to the general delivery and
> money-order windows. (June 15, 1899)

What with the growing summer population at the beaches in the north end of Port Huron, in August 1900 the city post office finally hired a mail carrier to deliver post to individual cottages:

> All residents at the beaches within the city limits who desire to
> have their mail delivered should have it addressed to the name
> of the beach where they are located, with the number or name
> of their cottage or hotel, otherwise prompt and certain delivery
> will not be possible. There will be two deliveries a day. (August
> 15, 1900)

You'd better write, or the folks back home might complain:

> "Ain't you got no paper?
> Ain't you got no pen?
> Ain't you got no envelope
> To put my letter in?" (July 30, 1944/TPB)

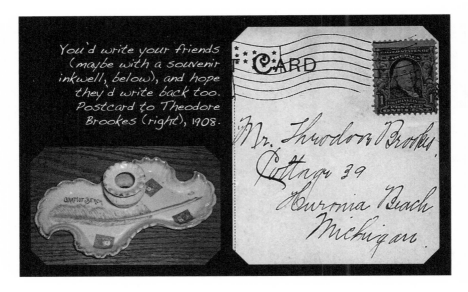

You'd write your friends (maybe with a souvenir inkwell, below), and hope they'd write back too. Postcard to Theodore Brookes (right), 1908.

Lolling and frolicking took a quantum leap for resorters in 1905 when local developers opened "Keewahdin Park," the amusement zone at the northern end of Gratiot Beach. Along with a dance hall and roller-skating rink, the place offered rides and sideshows for young and old alike, along with vaudeville acts in the theater and booze-free premises. Dubbed "the White City" from its prevailing paint scheme and countless electric lights, summers-only Keewahdin Park lasted barely a decade, closing at the end of the 1916 season and replaced by Gratiot Inn, as we have seen, once developers realized they could make more money from a hotel than an amusement park.

Some seven thousand eager townsfolk and resorters turned up for opening day of the park's 1907 season, which offered something for just about everyone:

> Vasser Cameroni, who will give exhibitions at Keewahdin Park
> next week, will slide down a high wire hanging by his teeth and
> will give a test of strength with a team of horses. (June 6, 1907)

John Guise, the female impersonator of the Burgess Stock company, has purchased the exclusive right to sell the souvenirs and novelties at Keewahdin park. (July 20, 1907)

A pier has been built out into the lake from Keewahdin park at which a launch, the Eunice, makes landings and takes parties for trips about the end of the lake. (July 6, 1907)

The wind and hail storm of Thursday apparently reached its greatest intensity in the neighborhood of Keewahdin park. Here "Maud," the "hit-and-get-a-cigar" mule broke loose from her fastenings and kicked the tent down. (August 3, 1907)

Summer 1915 saw the addition of the most famous ride of all at the park, the "Shoot the Chute" slide that dumped funsters in little toboggans out onto the lake:

The chute is forty-five feet high, has a slide of one hundred and fifty feet to the water, after which the boats will skim over the surface of the water for thirty feet. (July 14, 1915)

Entertainment choices, in between sliding down the Shoot the Chute. June 5, 1907.

Up North

Technology troubles could strike even in those low-tech days:

> We went up to Keewahdin to go on the Shoot the Chutes the other afternoon. It was lots of fun, but I wish they would get over the pernicious habit of putting heavy grease on the rollers, as it gets all over our hands and bathing suits. We got so bold that we went down lying down and backwards, but Theodore refused to follow Polly Bissell's example and go down standing up. The only excuse he could offer was that he had a family dependent upon him. (July 9, 1916/JIB)

> Took Mother and the girls up to Keewahdin Chutes this afternoon. Think Mother found the Chutes good fun but didn't care for the climb to the top. You will have to try them when you come. Charge admission to onlookers. (August 5, 1916/TPB)

Evening Magic

One of the joys of resort vacations was that every night was Saturday night. Something was always happening somewhere, from small gatherings to organized entertainments designed to appeal to a wide audience.

If you wanted more than just strolling the sidewalk of an evening, you could attend a musical performance, or a show of heaven knows what, sometimes for the benefit of charity:

> An entertainment will be given at Resort hall, Huronia, this evening for the benefit of Lakeside mission. A shadow pantomime, "Humpty Dumpty," "Alice in Wonderland," ballads and mandolin and guitar music will be given. (August 15, 1896)

The local minstrel troupe at the Windermere resort hall on Thursday evening had patrons from all the resorts between the lighthouse and Keewahdin. (August 19, 1899)

Miss Georgye Inslee, the child violinist, of Port Huron, will give a concert at Huronia hall, Friday evening, Aug. 17. Miss Inslee will be assisted by the Mozart Male Quartette, and Master Arthur Martin, boy soprano. (August 16, 1900)

The "Cutest Kids"
A week from tonight will be the date of one of the most novel masquerades ever thought of for the fun-loving beach people at Huronia. Young and old will go as children. Men will wear knee pants and women will wear their hair in braids and alter their gowns to appear childish. In the giving of prizes not only will dress be considered but childishness of manner will also count, and awards will go to the "cutest kids." (August 13, 1904)

Vaudeville at Huronia
Among the many entertainments which have been given at Huronia beach this season which have been so delightful was the vaudeville performance Thursday evening for the benefit of the Boys' Baseball club. . . . The program consisted of vocal solos by Miss Berhart, of Springfield; original songs by the "celebrated" Quince Orchestra of St. Louis; a number of good readings, and recitations for the pleasure of the children by Miss Welsher, of Topeka, Kansas; fancy dance by Miss Olga Bates, of St. Louis, and several good stories and vocal selections by Martin Ryan, of this city. (August 11, 1911)

An entertainment of "Living Pictures" and songs by a town trio
at the Dance Hall this evening. The pictures weren't so bad, but
singing was very poor and coarse. (July 23, 1914/JIB)

The Cabaret given at Gratiot hall last night will go on record as
one of the finest entertainments ever pulled off at Gratiot beach.
The hall was beautifully decorated in scarlet and black.

Crozier Lathrop of Detroit dressed as a Miss. Mr. Lathrop
looked so much like a girl in his evening costume with its up-to-
date cut, that even his closest friends were for a time deceived as
to his identity.

Senorita, a Mexican dancer, was impersonated by Mrs. Hickox
of Springfield, Ill.

The tango contest . . . was taken part in by six children,
dressed as older people would be for a like occasion. (August 8,
1914)

If live performers weren't available, a wind-up phonograph might do:

A victrola concert will be given in Gratiot beach hall Friday evening. (July 30, 1915)

How about improving your mind through informative lectures and presentations?

Capt. Samuel Alberti will give a series of stereopticon views on
Siberia, and also a collection of kinetoscope views, at the Windermere recreation hall on Thursday evening next. (July 16, 1898)

Prof. Vicary and Mrs. Jaccard, of the Vet Academy [music academy in Detroit] rendered a literary and musical program at the
hall at Huronia beach Wednesday evening. The attendance was
small. (July 30, 1898)

Or you could hie yourself downtown after supper to the Chautauquas, the itinerant presentations of lectures, cultural events, and musical performances wildly popular in America through the 1920s.

> Will & I went to the opening of the Redpath Chautauqua in
> afternoon & eve. Heard some good music by "Redpath Opera
> Co.," a quartet, & both times heard George McNutt ("The Dinner
> Pail Man") lecture. (August 1, 1913/ADGdiary)

> Chautauqua "Children's Night" tonight. First Bellini, an Italian
> player on the accordion, then a great cartoonist, then a magician
> and ventriloquist. Though nothing wonderful, they were amus-
> ing and the accordion playing quite novel. (August 5, 1914/JIB)

You might be invited down to the beach of an evening, for a hot time:

> Capt. E. J. Kendall built a mammoth fire on the beach at Kee-
> wahdin on Friday night and burned an effigy of Blanco, the
> Spanish general. (July 23, 1898, during the Spanish-American
> War)

One 1899 corn roast on the beach celebrated Mrs. Bert Duffie's birthday with a clever verse in the invitations:

> Next Friday is my birthday, friends—
> Don't ask how many years;
> If I should stop to count them up
> My eyes would fill with tears.
> Come gather 'round our cheerful fire
> And drink with me a toast;
> Just give the corn and taters—
> Instead of me—the roast. (July 29, 1899)

Weenie roasts could prove treacherous:

> Mrs. R. W. Emmens and Mrs. A. Weber entertained the Detroit
> residents at Huronia beach at a "hot dog" roast Wednesday eve-
> ning. Many of the guests complained, a few hours after eating,
> that the dogs were fighting among themselves, and physicians
> were in demand. (July 30, 1913)

If you were friends of the society set, you might be invited to a special
soiree:

> A party of people from Gratiot were guests of W. F. Davidson at
> a trolley party on Friday evening. The party occupied two of the
> City Railway company's large open cars, which were beautifully
> decorated with electric lights for the occasion. (August 1, 1896)

> The cake walk of Saturday evening last was originated by Mrs. R.
> S. Davis and Mrs. E. B. Norris. The cottagers at the Beaches have
> arranged a neat card of thanks for them in the form of a large
> card containing the signatures of about 50 people. It will be
> placed in a double frame and the reverse side will contain a view
> of the Windermere Hotel. (September 3, 1898)

Or just an old-fashioned party, perhaps with a theme and party stunts, if you
wanted to be fancy:

> Miss Katherine Hynson, of Huronia, gave a hat party in the hall
> Thursday evening at which prizes were awarded those who made
> the best paper hats. (August 3, 1904)

> Miss Julia Brookes gave a taffy-pull at her Huronia cottage Thurs-
> day night. (July 20, 1907)

> Unable to wait three more years, the young ladies of Huronia
> beach decided to give a leap year party. As one of the girls said

afterwards: "There were no wall flowers, unless they were men." (August 14, 1913)

Mrs. Southward's sheet and pillow-case party at nine this evening. We had a circle two-step, Virginia Reel etc. Then we un-masked and had ice cream, candy, and cake. We had a regular rough-house after most of the guests went home. The boys put ice down everyone's back. (July 27, 1914/JIB)

A Backward Party this evening for Dorothy and it certainly was fun. All the girls and boys wore their clothes backward, we served refreshments first, and the gentlemen first, we had a backward spelling match, and so forth. (August 19, 1914/JIB)

We went to the party. They had a number of guessing games and a drawing contest—each person was to draw a picture of his left-hand neighbor. . . . But the funniest thing was when Carrie and one of the men were given a suitcase and an umbrella. They were supposed to take two steps, open the umbrella, take two steps, close it, take two steps, open the suitcase and don the first article of apparel, close it, take two steps, open the umbrella, 2 steps, close it, 2 steps, open the suitcase, close it, 2 steps, open the umbrella, ad infinitum until all articles were put on and they had reached their starting point. It was a scream! I laughed until my sides ached and I couldn't laugh any more. We certainly had one whale of a good time and I was sorry you were not there. (August 14, 1923/AGB)

We had a backward spelling bee for a while and disposed of those who were too intelligent by giving them such words as transcendentalism and sesquicentennial. But after that all we could do was let them play games—such as Rook, Parcheesi, and Flinch, and finally offered them ginger ale and sandwiches and peanuts. Miss Mary Kingsley declined to play Rook on the ground that she wished to avoid even the appearance of evil, but as our cottage is secluded from the street and everyone on the place was at our house, I couldn't see how there was anyone who might be deceived by our appearance of playing cards. Even Ella the black cook calmly appeared and stayed for about ten minutes until shooed away with a bottle of ginger ale as a prize. Oh yes, we gave everyone the usual bag of twenty-five beans out of which he or she had to pay a forfeit of a bean every time he or she said yes or no, a device that seemed quite new to that company and kept them happy all evening. (JIB/August 5, 1926; the card game "Rook" wasn't considered really cards since it used its own deck, not a standard card deck)

Or a lavish birthday party:

One of the most enjoyable events of the season was the birthday banquet given Thursday evening by Oliver E. Connor to the "belles of the beach." Seventeen belles were present and dancing was enjoyed by all. Mr. Connor was the recipient of many presents. Supper was served à la Huronia style. The table decorations were lavender and pink sweet peas, and the dining room was beautifully decorated. (August 14, 1909)

But the great vogue in the evening, for the adult set, was after-dinner dancing. In the early years at Huronia, the dining hall was cleared of tables, the orchestra set up, and couples took to the floor. Tunes of dance orchestras filled the lakeshore air from Huronia's Resort Hall after its construction around 1893. Beachgoers invited young people from Port Huron too, not surprisingly since more than a few Huronia sojourners were townies themselves.

Resort hall at Huronia opened for the season on Friday evening. The London Harpers furnished the music for dancing. (July 2, 1898)

In the 1890s the debonair and limber could wow bystanders at the weekly evening hops, as they were called ("hop" usually denoting a less formal dance party, as opposed to a fancy dress ball), by attending Miss Gilby's dancing classes at Huronia on Tuesday afternoons. Once a month on Friday evenings a hop took place at Huronia, wildly popular events we know, as three hundred people (more than the entire population of Huronia) attended the dance held July 19, 1895. For a hop or ball, any theme was fair game:

> Wednesday evening, July 24, a fancy dress ball will be held at the dance hall. All present will dress like babies. (July 20, 1901/H)

> Saturday evening was the occasion of a masquerade ball at Huronia beach. Prizes were captured by Miss Lydia Lee for her character of "Carrie Nation" and Mr. Nelson in his make-up of "Mammy's Baby Girl." Mrs. Marcus Young assumed the character of "Uncle Sam." (August 21, 1903/H)

> A poverty ball will be given at Huronia dance hall this evening. Those who dress in the "raggiest rags" will be given prizes. (August 6, 1904)

Soon enough, *every* night was dance night at the Beaches—not surprisingly, since everyone at the resorts was on vacation and up for entertainment of an evening. The one exception—of course!—was Sunday: no dancing on the Sabbath.

Fancier dances in those prewar years were "germans," cotillions that featured the elaborate social dance of that name. So along with swimming suits, resorters had to pack their fancy duds in their trunks, if they planned on making a splash in the evenings too:

> About 300 people attended the german Saturday evening at Resort hall. . . . Favors included Japanese fans, parasols, boats,

flowers, compass and chain, and Merry Widow ruffles. (July 18, 1908)

The favor cotillion given at Huronia beach Saturday evening . . . was one of the most delightful and beautiful affairs which has ever been given during the history of this resort. The hall was crowded with four hundred onlookers, resorters, and Port Huron residents who watched with delight the cotillion which was participated in by thirty-six couples, led by Miss Mabel Strauss, of St. Louis, and George McLaughlin, also of St. Louis. . . . The sight was made attractive by the beautiful gowns worn by the lovely young girls who took part in the dancing, while the favors presented to the dancers were unique, pretty, and comical. (July 31, 1911)

Were there enough boys to go around? Maybe not:

An Adamless Eden.
Cold truth compels the confession that Huronia Beach is a sort of Adamless Eden. . . . The mammas and the children flock here in full force, while *pater familias* guards the lonesome home, does business at the old stand, sends to his better half his compliments and regrets and his checks, while he seeks consolation on the bleaching boards of the ball game and dry lunches of the club. An estimate, the accuracy of which would put a census enumerator to blush, gives this beach at this time 200 children, 150 maids, matrons, and grandmothers, nurses to match, and say fifty members, all told, of the *genus homo*. An equal number of the sexes places the male at a par value, as the relation stands here under existing circumstances, a man is an extravagant premium, say 200 to 300 percent. . . . It permits ample opportunity not only for the heroic, but for the observation and cultivation of that delightful and perplexing study: woman, who, Pope declares, "is at best a contradiction still." Well, if the acute poet

were summering at Huronia, he would not find her very still.
(August 20, 1890)

How to rectify the scarcity of young gents?

> The summer resort keepers ought to get leave of absence for the
> West Point cadets and then distribute them through the country,
> so that summer girls will have somebody to dance with. (June
> 13, 1895)

Only a few years later the shoe was on the other dancing foot:

> The gentlemen are in the majority among the young people at both
> Gratiot and Huronia and the ladies are at a premium. (July 31, 1899)

One major purpose of all the socializing was to expose marriageable young
adults to one another. Mightn't the two-step or the tennis match lead, just
possibly, to matrimony?

> One of the notable engagements of the fall season is that of Miss
> Theotiste Nugent to Leon S. Herbert of Philadelphia. . . . Miss
> Nugent met her fiancé six years ago at Gratiot Beach, Mich., where
> they were both spending the summer. (September 29, 1918/SLPD)

For some, the real reason for vacationing. July 19, 1895.

Up North

You never knew if summer merrymaking would meet expectations:

> The dances at Gratiot hall are rather poorly attended. A stroll on the beach seems preferable to "tipping the light fantastic toe." (July 23, 1903)

> Sat around boredly at the Dancing Hall this evening. There was practically no one there except a Gratiot couple or two. Poor Mrs. Dean nearly goes crazy trying to make people come in and dance. (July 1, 1914/JIB)

> I never was cut out for a social pirate, and I wish Ma wouldn't keep poking strange people off on me. Mrs. Dean introduced Ma to a Cauter family who had just come from St. Louis and Mother insisted that I go see the girl of the family. I'd never even seen her, and she was much nearer the age of either Lib or Katharine, but because they had mentioned tennis, I was the one selected to be butchered to make a Roman holiday. Just imagine what opinion they must have had of a perfect stranger's mentality who came stalking in on them while they were unpacking. Well, I survived it, and they seem to have too. I was somewhat reconciled by the thought that I would have someone to play tennis with; but when she and brother Francis and I played the next morning, I found that they had only started to learn last summer, so they don't do me any good—hardly. (July 9, 1916/ JIB)

To Veg, or Not to Veg

If none of the plentiful activities at the Beaches rang your bell, you could just stagnate around the cottage all day.

Porch canvas swings made good perches for lake gazing.
Julia Brookes and nephews, Huronia, 1914.

A little sewing and reading today, but really nothing exciting
doing. We just sat around and thought. (July 30, 1914/JIB)

You didn't have to do anything fancy in the evening either.

The present warm evenings make the entire line of the beaches
a place of attractive rest and pleasure for cottagers, who occupy
their verandas in large numbers. A large number of rowboats
on the lake also add a wonderful beauty to the scene. (July 17,
1895)

We got a rug and sat on the beach and watched shooting stars
till ten o'clock. We sang what few hymns we knew as we lay.
(August 16, 1914/JIB)

Uncle Brown handed us the Family Letter a few days ago, and
we read it aloud last evening. In a summer cottage, where peo-

ple are going & coming so much, it is hard to find a time when
all are together, unoccupied. (September 11, 1915/ADG)

Mrs. Scott is one of those charming and deceptively reticent folks
of Scotch origin. The folks tried to show her some Brookes tricks
at Rook last evening. Does she learn fast! (August 13, 1944/TPB)

Vacation it might be, but if you owned your cottage rather than rented, you
had to set up housekeeping just like at home. One might wonder from her
diary whether Gratiot cottager Ada Greene really considered herself on vacation, but she certainly would have said she did:

Mr. Tracey came this A.M. to give me his bid for repairs, then I
had to go to town in the P.M. to get a draft for Agnes. Bought
lawn mower. City Laundry man called. Port Huron Creamery
brought milk & will do so every other day. — Ice man gave us
ice today. Fannie & I weeded the grass & started on lawn this
A.M., before the rain. — Raked lawn & changed hose — Pulled
up & cut down grape vine on elm tree. Carpenter stopped in,
sat quite a while. Another ice man came. — Finished & tacked
down dining room carpet. — This morning we took some
earth down and planted our flowers in the boxes. — Starched
& stretched curtains. Ironed curtains, cut out draperies & box
coverings & Fannie sewed some on them. — Plumber came and
looked over ground for cesspool. — Painters began this A.M.,
three men working. Carpenter botched bay window; discharged
him, having promise of another man tomorrow. — Four painters all day, finished all but oiling floors inside, took ladders
away. — Plumber came at 6:30 A.M. to fix closet. Had a flare-
up on gas stove. We put up curtains, sewed dining room rug,
laid other rugs, & by six had it in pretty good shape. Painters
oiled kitchen, dining room, & bathroom floors & painted the
back. — Clark & I stuffed feather pillows, covered washstand,

burned papers & went to town on 9:30 car. — After morning
work, trimmed grape vines & cut weeds about the house. —
Got breakfast on electric toaster, swept out, washed a few dishes
& cut a path of grass. — I went to town 8:30 to see about
heater for water boiler. Later I met Clark & we bought a Victrola
and an oil cook stove. — Ruth & Eloise came down in A.M., we
hung some curtains, mended etc. I went to town in P.M., looked
at iron bed with springs, 3 cotton mattresses & a few chairs.
Agnes & Ruth ironed & hung curtains. Had Mr. Young haul bed
and take away old mattresses. — Clark put mosquito netting on
little windows today. — Swept upstairs, made 4 glasses currant
jelly & some raspberry jam. — Busy about house in A.M. Went
to town in P.M., paid bills, & other errands. Mrs. Scott over
in eve. I made butter with dover egg beater from 1 pt. sour
cream. — Washed some curtains in eve, boiling on oil stove
in living room as we needed it for heat. — We ironed Ruth's
clothes, which arrived from laundry after she left. (May 22, 23,
24, 1911; June 1, 7,8, 20, 1911; August 16, 1911; May 9, 27,
30, 1912; June 1, 3, 1912; August 3, 1912; June 21, 1913;
July 5, 9, 15, 26, 1913; August 30, 1913; May 25, 1915;
August 7, 1915/ADGdiary)

Even if your family rented its cottage, Mother wouldn't let you forget about chores:

Sweeping day for me. Ye gods but I'm tired of being house-maid
and laundress and general maid-of-all-work all summer! (July
20, 1914/JIB)

Housework finished, or if you were lucky enough not to have any, you might indulge in the time-honored occupation of contemplating the panorama of lake and sky. The mystery, then as now, is why loafing vacationers seem perpetually both drowsy and hungry.

Hanging out at Huronia Beach. Mrs. Brookes and Mrs. Samuel of St. Louis, 1905.

> A guest at the Windermere said on Thursday, "I've sat here in sight of Lake Huron for an hour, enjoying a glorious rest, but I'm wondering where it was that I got such an appetite." (July 3, 1896)

Midwestern thunderstorms could liven things up.

> Talk about downpours, last Tuesday we had a severe electrical storm. The family was serenely sleeping when all of a sudden the wind began blowing, accompanied by thunder and lightning. No sooner were the windows shut than the rain came down in all its fury. (July 31, 1927/TPBJr)

> Agnes and I sat on the porch listening to the rain on the roof, admiring a rainbow in the southeast. (August 6, 1944/TPB)

Sometimes rainstorms could decide cottagers to head for home, as with the four young ladies at Huronia in 1902 who, with their chaperone, called themselves the Illahee Club:

O Illahee! O Illahee!
My heart most fondly goes with thee,
While wearily on my homeward way
My "footsies" take me this wet day.
I would so gladly go, with "Lill"
And of your food eat my good fill,
But from the clouds there comes a pour
That turns my steps way from your door.
I send my love and do regret
The powers have made it so awful wet. (August 9, 1902)

Regardless of how you spent your days or what the weather brought, the goal was to let your summertime setting work its magic:

Rev. Dr. A. B. Riggs, of Cincinnati: "The present season has been one of the most delightful that myself and family have ever spent at the Beach. I came from home very weary from my year's work, but have rapidly recuperated in the midst of these refreshing Lake Huron breezes." (August 20, 1898)

Relaxing in the summer sun: Sue and May Siebert of Columbus, Elsie Riggs and Helen Taylor of Cincinnati, and unidentified companion, ca. 1902.

Up North

Looking back from 1936, two St. Louis sisters at Gratiot remembered Huronia in its heyday:

> There were about 60 cottages there and three-fourths of them
> were occupied by St. Louis people. We used to have grand times
> in those days. There was a dance pavilion where they had enter-
> tainers, cotillions, and other activities. We used to have roasts on
> the beach and all sorts of fun. . . . (September 3, 1936)

All in all the fun-filled summer days of youth at the Beaches could look pretty rosy in the rear-view mirror of life . . .

> What a long time has elapsed since 1906! Sometimes as I look
> at the young people who are the beaus and belles of the beach
> now I wish that time might turn back for a little and that we
> might have a few of those happy days again.

. . . until one snapped out of the dreamy wistfulness:

> However, they can't begin to come up to our present happiness.
> (August 21, 1920/AGB, Agnes writing to her husband Theodore,
> the two having become engaged at the Beach in 1906)

Chapter 6
Chapel Bells

Upright, churchgoing resorters were supposed to attend church on Sunday even during summer holidays, a custom my grandmother Agnes adhered to, well, religiously, throughout her life. By the time I spent the summer of 1959 at the cottage with her, she had switched from the Presbyterian to the more conservative Baptist church in downtown Port Huron. Of worship services with her that summer I recall nothing at all, typical of a nine-year-old. But I have a still-vivid memory of one Sunday evening fellowship dinner—Sloppy Joes washed down with orange soda pop, which led to disastrous consequences for me back in the cottage during the night, and the inability to countenance the mere mention of that particular culinary combination for the rest of my life, even now.

But most resorters at old-time Huronia and Gratiot didn't have to tear themselves away from the lake of a Sunday morning to go into town to church, since a chapel to accommodate the summer crowds went up right there at the Beach. What with Huronia and Gratiot overwhelmingly Protestant, the Beach chapel too was Protestant, and nondenominational to encourage the largest possible congregation.

Pious Huronia beacher Henry I. Armstrong of Detroit, himself a Presbyterian, spearheaded the chapel's creation when in late 1888 he purchased a small rectangular chunk out of the far northwest corner of Huronia Beach property for a chapel. No doubt Mr. Young agreed to sell the lot to Mr. Armstrong because its distance from the lake made the location relatively unsuitable for a revenue-generating cottage, or so it seemed at the time. The chapel went up the next spring, in 1889:

> During the summer divine services will be held at Huronia Beach
> every Sunday. The new chapel is a beauty. (June 12, 1889)

With its elegant short steeple and shutters at the windows, the pretty white clapboard building looked straight out of New England.

Though he'd led the charge to equip the Beaches with a house of worship, when it came to naming it Mr. Armstrong ceded the honor to the memory of Mrs. Elizabeth Dean, whose cottage stood close to his own. The pioneer Gratiot resorter, herself a widow, had died of cancer in Cincinnati in January 1891 at the age of fifty-one, leaving five young children. Her death may have particularly shocked Gratiot Beach folk because as near as one can tell Mrs. Dean was the first cottager at the fledgling resort to die.

> Mrs. Dean . . . will be remembered as having constructed in
> 1886 the first cottage at Gratiot Beach and Dean memorial chap-
> el is named in her honor. (July 8, 1893)

Dean Memorial Chapel (as the scroll above the porch proclaims), right next door to Huronia's cottage #60.

Other beachers contributed to the place, according to their talents:

> A Mr. Finney of Gratiot carved a pulpit for the Chapel last sum-
> mer, and now he has made a bench to match for the preacher's
> seat. Mrs. Lindenberg, daughter of Mr. Townsend, gave the
> cushion. (July 12, 1908/MPB)

Who preached at this summer chapel? Fellow resorters—Protestant ministers
on vacation at the Beaches who didn't mind working while on holiday. Re-
lying upon vacationing pastors meant the chapel didn't open for the season
until one of them arrived who could be talked into overseeing services.

> Sabbath. Another hot day. First preaching service of the season
> in the chapel, led by a brother-in-law of Mrs. Bull, Dr. Gray of
> Greenville, Tenn. Text Micah. (July 9, 1911/ADGdiary)

Until such a minister showed up for his "vacation," and after all likely candi-
dates had departed in August or September, observant resorters had to head
into town on Sunday mornings.

Mr. Armstrong's father-in-law, the Reverend William Aikman of Atlantic
City, New Jersey, not only preached at Dean Chapel, he published an article
entitled "Gratiot Beach" in 1900 in the journal of his calling. The good minister approved of the Gratiot crowd, as he told his readers in appropriately
ministerial-sounding language:

> The summer—there is no winter—company that gathers here
> is a choice one. They come from the churches of Michigan,
> Ohio, Kentucky, and Missouri, mostly . . . Professor Morris, late
> of Lane Theological Seminary was wont to resort thither, and
> this summer, on the porch of his pretty cottage, I talked with
> Dr. Riggs—"shop," I am sorry to say—that is, New Testament
> Greek, which he teaches at Lane. Last year on our own piazza
> I discussed the Atlanta campaign of our Civil War with General
> Cox, soldier and accomplished writer, whose recent death we

mourn. Then there are college girls and boys from Vassar and
Bryn Mawr and Swarthmore and Michigan University, who make
jolly companions of weekdays and an audience which is a joy to
preach to on Sundays.

We have a pretty chapel here—"Dean Memorial," as it is
called. It is one of the privileges of the year to preach from
Sabbath to Sabbath in it. The eager listening of the young and
old that fill it, the distant murmur of the lake, the light of the
sunshine through the trees, the breeze that whispers through
the blinds shading the open windows, all make a memory that
lasts delightfully through the year. As we walk toward the chapel
under the trees, the verse of Montgomery's comes up:

To Thy temple I repair,
Lord, I love to worship there
When within the veil I meet
Christ before the mercy seat.[20]

It is good there to sing and pray and preach. (*New York
Evangelist*, October 25, 1900)

The Dr. Riggs on whose cottage porch Rev. Aikman discussed New Testament
Greek was to prove by far the most frequent preacher at the chapel. Rev.
Alexander Brown Riggs of Cincinnati vacationed with his family at Huronia
before building his own cottage at Gratiot in 1895. The reverend became
a familiar fixture of the Beach, preaching at Dean Chapel every summer
from 1893 through 1919, the year of his death at age seventy-seven. Given
that vacationing pastors usually enjoyed long vacations, like schoolchildren,
cottagers could count on Dr. Riggs to take the pulpit most Sundays of the
season, once he arrived at the Beach.

Dr. Riggs preached to a good congregation this morning, on
Hebrews 2:10. He expects to speak on Hebrews all summer.
(July 12, 1908/MPB)

Gratiot cottager Rev. Alexander Brown Riggs of the Seventh Presbyterian Church in Cincinnati preached at the chapel every summer for twenty-seven years, until his death in 1919.

> Dr. Riggs announced that next Sunday would be his last service of this season. That makes one feel as though the summer was almost over. (August 11, 1912/MPB)

At season's height, one had the choice of three chapel "activities" to attend each Sabbath:

> Rev. A. B. Riggs, of Cincinnati, will preach at the Dean chapel on Sunnay morning. Sunday school will follow the service and the usual praise service in the evening, led by Mr. Strelinger. (August 15, 1896)

Hymn singing, usually to piano accompaniment, would raise the rafters at Sunday morning services.

> Sabbath. First service in chapel. Uncle Brown preached, I played for the hymns. Kate, May & Lucy Riggs sang twice, without an accompaniment. It was a beautiful service. (July 18, 1915/ADG-diary, Ada Greene being Rev. Riggs's niece)

Apparently the steeple had a bell, or else the dining hall bell served to summon you up from the beach for worship:

> The first bell is ringing for song service so shall close this letter
> with love. (July 29, 1906/TPB)

Even pastors risk judgment by the fickle public:

> Chapel services have been very well attended each Sunday this
> month. Dr. Riggs has promised to continue them through the
> month. His subjects this year have been a little less doctrinal
> than usual and more practical, it seems. No doubt Mother
> has told you of the condescension which led the Kochigs to
> pronounce Dr. Riggs actually intelligent and even cultured. I
> presume they had expected to find a country pastor in charge of
> a tiny rural chapel. (August 17, 1913/TPB)

Youngsters could be irreverent chapelgoers, unless imitation is indeed the sincerest flattery:

> I came out on the porch to write and found the chairs lined up
> in rows and Louise very anxious to show me a seat. I took one
> and she immediately took the rostrum and repeated Dr. Riggs's
> morning sermon verbatim. I declare, if that girl didn't look after
> this family it would certainly go to wrack and ruin, according to
> her ideas anyway. (July 12, 1906/TPB; Louise Brookes being four
> years old at the time)

Dr. Riggs had made such a splash at the Beaches that when he died in Cincinnati in September 1919, the Port Huron paper of September 11 ran an item on his life since, as the tagline announced, "Well Known Divine Had Spent Summers At Beaches For Years."

Who funded the chapel? Wealthy donors no doubt, and the Sunday collection plate would've helped. Charity benefits also assisted, starting with this effort to raise funds while the chapel still lay on the planning boards:

A children's fair for the benefit of the chapel will be held at the Windermere, Gratiot Beach, on Wednesday of next week, August 1, afternoon and evening. Ten cents admission will be charged. Streetcars will run to accommodate Port Huron patrons. (July 28 and 31, 1888)

Later benefits, such as this one of 1895, reached cultural heights with recitals of Grieg, Schubert, Saint-Saëns, and Bizet:

A most delightful musicale was given last night at Gratiot Beach, at the cottage of Mr. H. I. Armstrong, for the benefit of the chapel fund. The program was rendered by Mr. and Mrs. Amor W. Sharp, of Columbus, Ohio, with Miss Ransom, of Detroit, as accompanist. . . . Mrs. Sharp has a high, robust soprano of beautiful quality. . . . Mr. Sharp's bass-baritone is round, rich and even from top to bottom. . . . (July 30, 1895)

Less lofty endeavors also kept the house of worship in the black:

A bazaar is announced to be held at the Gratiot "Casino" on Thursday, Aug. 11th, from 4 to 9:30 p.m. The proceeds will go to the support of the Dean chapel. The funds will be used in repainting the building. (July 30 and August 6, 1898)

Mother took the children down to a marshmallow roast at the Finneys. It was a pay affair which the children had gotten up for the benefit of the Chapel—ten cents a person. They cleared over $6.00. (August 20, 1920/AGB)

At least one church in town gave Dean Chapel some competition:

Rev. John Munday will bring his Grace church cadets to the Windermere resort hall on Thursday evening next. They will give some very pretty exhibition drills and other items of interest will be on the program. (July 26, 1902)

Other church congregations might furnish an unexpected sight, if you saun-
tered down the beach far enough:

> Men, women and children, old and young and middle-aged,
> gathered in the vicinity of the lighthouse Wednesday afternoon,
> to witness the baptismal rites of the Mennonite church. Without
> doubt a large percentage of the crowd had gathered solely out
> of curiosity, and to them the affair was only a show at which
> they laughed, when it pleased their fancy, and criticised indis-
> criminately at other times.
>
> There were 14 people to be baptised and they were taken one
> at a time. The two elders would lead the candidate into the lake
> several feet from shore, while the brethren and sisters on the
> shore joined in singing. Standing in the water to their waists, the
> elders would proceed with the ceremony, which concluded in
> each instance with the immersion of the convert. The water was
> far from warm and the ceremony was usually followed by much
> chattering of teeth. (August 30, 1900)

> The pastor is a Baptist but serving in a non-denominational
> tabernacle he has no baptistry. So he announced baptismal
> services this afternoon on the beach right next to the Riggs
> cottage. Have heard no reports of any difficulty, so no doubt all
> went well. Personally I'd rather a baptism be more private and
> less of a display before a gawking public. But that is their affair.
> (August 13, 1944/TPB)

Besides attending Dean Chapel or heading into town on Sundays, pious resorters could tend to spiritual needs at the annual interdenominational Bible
conference, organized around 1914 along north Gratiot Beach:

> The Keewahdin Bible conference opens July 11 and continues
> until the 16th inclusive. A tabernacle, which will seat five hundred

people, has been erected by Mrs. Starcke. . . . The tabernacle is
so constructed that it can be closed on stormy days and the sides
thrown open when the weather permits. (July 7, 1916)

"Bring Your Bibles and Friends" and "Come Praying," exhorted the brochure for the weeklong conference, which remained a beach fixture into the 1920s. But when organizers wearied of the task after the 1928 season, the tabernacle closed, and that ended Bible school on the Beach.

Looks like nature had no respect for Bible Conference worshipers:

We had a song service and Scripture lesson by Miss Page last
night. Poor Agnes was standing in front, leading the singing.
She did nobly, in spite of her frantic efforts to keep off the
mosquitoes. When she called on Miss Kingsley for a solo, she
reached promptly for my bottle of Citronella. Miss Carrie began
bravely, but in the midst of the first verse there must have been
a particularly vicious jab, for she faltered, stopped, and with an
apology, went on. (September 7, 1926/MPB)

Not everyone was thrilled with the Beach Sunday experience, which dictated that proper young ladies and gentlemen were to respect the Sabbath by not cavorting as they did during the week:

To the Chapel as usual this morning, and bored as usual. Wrote
a letter to father this afternoon and then read for the rest of
the time. Read "The Fortunate Youth" to Elizabeth and Julia this
evening, then went to bed about half past nine. Sunday certainly
is boredom personified. (August 2, 1914/JIB)

My sweeping day today, then chapel. Oh! Just as usual. A missionary man—cruel creature—spoke for forty minutes in spite of
the heat, and we barely got home in time for dinner. (August 9,
1914/JIB)

Teenagers might be bored, but chapel still gave them the opportunity to gussy up:

> Sweeping today, then up to the chapel as usual. I was a fetching symphony in lavender—dress, stockings, ribbon, pendant, beauty pin, and Julia's lavender hat. (July 26, 1914/JIB)

Chapelgoing was one activity the whole family participated in while on vacation.

> Louise did a little thing in chapel that touched me very much. She pointed to the word "love" at the top of the page, and then snuggled up to me, squeezing my arm to show its meaning. (August 11, 1912/MPB)

Churchgoing on Sunday was so expected in some quarters, despite being on vacation, that *not* going called for creative excuses, even to one's own diary:

> Sabbath. A perfect day. Kitchen arrangements so crude, gasoline stove poor & hands sore with poison ivy, took a long time to get breakfast, so decided not to go to church. (June 18, 1911/ ADGdiary)

> Sabbath. Not knowing car service, and as it was raining, no one tried to go to church. (May 5, 1912/ADGdiary)

> Sabbath. It was 9:30 before dishes were washed, so did not attempt to go to church. (May 19, 1912/ADGdiary).

> Raining this A.M., baby fussy so it was too late by the time breakfast was over to get ready for church. (September 15, 1912/ADGdiary)

> Sabbath. Had breakfast too late to go to town to church & there
> is no service on the Beach, so we all stayed at home. (July 13,
> 1913/ADGdiary)

In addition to Sunday worship services, the Huronia chapel hosted at least one funeral, that of Marcus Young, on August 19, 1913. As fate would have it the founder of Huronia died in summer, so that his funeral could be attended by the resorters who had benefited from his vision, with services led by the chapel's preeminent preacher, Rev. Riggs himself.

> At 2:30 I attended the funeral service of Marcus Young in the
> Chapel, conducted by Uncle Brown. (August 19, 1913/ADGdiary)

After the service the congregation followed the casket across the road to Lakeside Cemetery, where Mr. Young was laid to rest atop a knoll within sight of the resort he'd created.

The chapel could also serve any number of other purposes, not just religious:

> The Misses Dwyer are holding an exhibition of watercolors and
> hand-painted china at the Dean chapel, at Huronia beach. . . . A
> very beautifully executed piece is an illustration from the Court-
> ship of Miles Standish. (August 15, 1895)

> Ladies from the Beaches met at the Dean chapel this morning to
> arrange for meetings at which sewing will be done for wounded
> soldiers in the Cuban war. (July 22, 1898)

> Major Fechet is to deliver his famous lecture on the "Indians in the
> West" at the Dean chapel on Monday evening. (July 26, 1902)

When Huronia Beach closed down in 1919, the chapel lost a good deal of its raison d'être. With the Huronia cottages demolished or hauled away, and

Deserted survivor: the silent chapel in August 1920, the year after Huronia Beach closed.

other summer folk now reaching downtown Port Huron churches by car, the chapel stood off by itself at its lonely corner throughout the 1920s. Though advancing in years, Henry Armstrong understandably had no wish to see his generous deed of 1888 come to naught, and so the wrecker's ball was stayed. Not that buyers were beating down his door, since the small plot of land didn't overlook the lake and so wouldn't exactly attract offers to buy.

Even though Dean Chapel no longer resounded with sermon and hymns of a Sunday morning after Huronia Beach went out of business, through the 1920s some Gratiot resorters soldiered on in the otherwise deserted house of prayer for occasional "sing-outs" on Sunday evenings. My father said that ladies, including his mother Agnes, would scrub the place out and set it right for these events, which required no preacher.[21]

We have been going down to Song Service each Sunday night.
One woman has been making very simple, beautiful prayers for
the children. Each night before praying she asks the children
for what they are thankful. One day Bobby's hand went up and
she asked him. He said, "I'm thankful for doctors who keep us
well." I nearly snorted aloud. That was the same Sunday evening
that Mrs. Finney sent for me to lead the singing, as she was not
feeling well. I did it, though didn't want to much. (August 30,
1921/AGB; Agnes's husband Theodore was a doctor, and though
she couldn't have known it when she wrote this letter, their son
Bobby became a physician too when he grew up.)

The end came in September 1931, during the Depression, when with his
shaky signature Mr. Armstrong—eighty years old at the time, a widower, but
still owner of the chapel lot after forty-three years—deeded the land to the
owner of all the rest of the former Huronia Beach site surrounding it. The
pretty wooden tabernacle must have fallen to the wreckers soon afterward,
as it disappeared from city directories the following year.

Even all these decades later, long after anyone who could have known it
has passed away, there's something poignant about the death of the deserted chapel that witnessed so many sermons and prayers and hymns over the
summers, and at least one funeral. Now it was permanently silenced. Like
summer vacations, its time had ended. The world moved on.

Chapter 7
Mishap, Misadventure, and Woe

Resort promoters wouldn't mention it, but summertime fun could turn sour too, even tragic. For one thing, however the food was at the dining halls and hotels, could you get sick from the water? Thanks to advances in understanding disease transmission, by 1882 newspapers advised the resort-going public to ponder not only the various amusements advertised at summer resorts but also the state of sewer drainage, due to "the close connection which is now generally believed to exist between such diseases as typhoid fever, diarrhoea, diphtheria, etc., and methods of sewage disposal."[22] We don't know Huronia's provision for waste disposal, but quite likely it resembled the "village method of water supply and disposal of excreta" that the local paper warned resorters against:

> We advise our readers to look before they leap, for to leave
> one's comfortable city home in pursuit of health and pleasure,
> and contract typhoid as the result, is too much like going out to
> look for wool and coming back shorn. (September 6, 1882)

At least Lake Huron offered one bright side to the laissez-faire waste disposal of the day:

> The current down the lake from the Corsica shoals is of such a
> character as to carry past the lower beaches all refuse in the lake,
> and dead fish or other driftings are very seldom seen. (June 16,
> 1900)

In those days epidemics could be deadly. Huronia had its scares:

> Whooping cough has appeared in several families at Huronia
> Beach and Manager Young fears a general stampede in conse-

quence. Several families left today and more will follow to-morrow. Mothers seem to fear the disease and have telegraphed their husbands for instructions. (August 24, 1886)

Notwithstanding the parties who had the whooping cough have returned to their homes, eight more families left Huronia Beach this morning. What they are leaving for is beyond the comprehension of Manager Young. (August 26, 1886)

One can understand the concern, as death was never remote in the nineteenth century, even at holiday retreats.

A little son of Mr. and Mrs. Elwood died at Huronia Beach Tuesday. This is the first death that has occurred at that resort. (September 10, 1886)

Mrs. Cornelia Howard Strong, of Detroit, who has been stopping at Huronia Beach with her daughter for some time past, died on Sunday morning at 3 o'clock, aged 68 years. The remains were shipped to Detroit on Sunday. (August 19, 1889)

Geo. S. Scarlett, the one-year-old son of Wm. Scarlett, died at Gratiot Beach this morning. The remains will be taken to Columbus, Ohio, for burial on Tuesday morning. (September 2, 1895)

Shimmering in the sun on warm summer days, Lake Huron looked peaceful and inviting and completely harmless. Mostly, it was.

Geo. S. Ward, a visitor at Huronia beach, expressed himself to a *Times* reporter on Friday afternoon as follows: "Did you ever notice how free this place has been from accidents and casualties? From the number of little children who play on the shore of the lake it is a surprise that there are no drownings to record.

Yet I am told that no such accidents have happened during the
history of the beach." (August 6, 1892)

But for the unwary the peaceful lake could turn treacherous, and such optimism proved a bit premature, alas:

DROWNED

Willie T. Sherman, the 12-year-old son of L. A. Sherman, of
The Times, was drowned in front of John W. Porter's cottage, at
Huronia Beach, at 11 o'clock this forenoon. In company with
Harry and Rodger Wheeler, two young companions, he was
bathing in the lake. Willie started to swim out to a diving board.
When about half way to the board he was evidently seized
with cramps. He was noticed to throw up his hands, call for
assistance, and then sink. The boys at once called several men in
the vicinity, but they were unable to render any assistance as the
drowning boy had disappeared beneath the surface of the water
before their arrival. Up to the time *The Times* went to press the
body had not been recovered. (August 31, 1894)

DROWNED AT HURONIA
Edward M. Kanter, of Detroit, Seized with
Cramps While in Bathing—Efforts to
Save His Life Unavailing.
. . . Mr. Kanter came to Port Huron on Wednesday evening to
spend a few days at his mother's cottage. About four o'clock on
Thursday he concluded to go in bathing. Suddenly his friends
missed him, but it was believed he had dived into the water. At
the end of a few moments, however, all was excitement and an
effort was made to recover the body. It was found in a bent position on the bottom of the lake in about six feet of water. Every
effort was made by the people at the beach to bring about re-
suscitation and the life-saving crew worked over him for an hour.
He was evidently dead when taken from the water. Mrs. Kanter,

the mother, watched the efforts to save her son and when he was pronounced dead her grief was pitiable. (July 25, 1902)

Suppose you have had many accounts of the tragedy last Sunday. From the history and failure of resuscitory efforts I advanced the theory of fainting or death before the girl fell from the canoe. It seems to have been generally adopted and as I doubt if the coroner held an autopsy it will no doubt stand. (August 1, 1916/TPB)

Cramps were a frightening peril parents warned against. The standard rule along the beaches, transmitted down the generations, was no swimming for one hour after eating.

Celia has brought in the tragic news that a soldier, home on furlough, drowned up near the Bang cottage early this afternoon. It was the same old story, he ate a hearty dinner and then went swimming. We have not the details but it is to be presumed he had the usual cramps and went down. These hearts of ours are wonderful pumps but should not be imposed upon by combining a full stomach, heavy exercise, and cold water all at once. (September 5, 1943/TPB)

No swimming after eating: Bert Riggs (son of Rev. Riggs), Bertha Dunlap, Clark Greene, Ada Greene, Nellie Dunlap, Mr. Engle, Howard Dunlap (brother of Ada), Theodore Brookes, 1906.

Some close calls had happy endings:

> Mrs. L. Wilbur Crane, of Springfield, O., whose little son was
> saved from drowning some days ago by Robert Nelson, has
> made Mrs. Nelson and her son some very substantial cash gifts
> in memory of the young man's deed. (September 4, 1897)

One young cottager netted the Silver Medal of the United States Life-Saving
Service for his heroic deed in 1893:

> Name: George B. Dean, Cincinnati, Ohio—Service Rendered:
> Rescued, on July 17, 1893, at Gratiot Beach, Lake Huron, a
> youth who sank to the bottom while bathing about 100 yards
> offshore. The rescue was effected at great personal risk by diving
> and supporting the unconscious boy until both were taken from
> the water by boatmen.[23]

Sometimes the lake wasn't as dangerous as it seemed, though:

> Ed. J. Kendall saved the life of Dennis P. Sullivan on Sunday af-
> ternoon. Mr. Sullivan went in bathing at the beach. He is unable
> to swim, and to be on the safe side, took a rowboat with him as
> he ventured out into the lake. For an hour he splashed around
> in the water, hanging onto the stern of the boat. Suddenly
> those on shore heard a piercing scream and looking out on Lake
> Huron discovered that Denny had lost his hold on the boat. He
> was making a brave effort to keep his head above water and
> calling loudly for help. His head was going under water for the
> third time when Ed. J. Kendall, who was in the vicinity with a
> rowboat, went to the rescue. As the boat neared the drowning
> man, Mr. Kendall yelled:
>
> "Stand up Denny, stand up! You are not in deep water."
>
> Sullivan took heart. He placed his feet on the sandy bottom and
> stood up. By actual measurement the water was 17½ inches deep.

Mr. Sullivan, in trembling tones, thanked Mr. Kendall for the great service rendered. The attorney will hereafter confine his bathing to a bath tub. (September 6, 1897)

Perhaps the lesson is, don't almost drown when there's someone around who will blab to the newspaper.

Pranks were not out of the question at the family resort:

On Tuesday afternoon a number of boys at Gratiot Beach were shooting at a mark. One of the bullets glanced off and entered the cottage of Mrs. Frank Shaw, striking her little granddaughter, Lucille Stockman, in the shoulder. The wound is painful, but not serious. (July 31, 1895)

BEACH JOKES
— —

College Boys Bring Their Love of Fun Along.

Many of the young men at the beaches are college fellows and when they come here for the summer they do not leave their propensity for practical jokes at home and someone is sure to suffer. A few nights ago at Gratiot beach a young man happened to be alone all night in a cottage. Some of his friends were aware of this and they entered the house in the dead of night and put carbon bi-sulphide in the room. The obnoxious odor soon drove the young fellow from the house and he had to take refuge in the wood shed. On another occasion a young fellow was carried from his bed in the middle of the night and given a ducking in the cool waters of the lake. (September 4, 1903/H)

MAN WITH A BLACK CAPE
— —

Annoyed Young Ladies at Beaches Thursday Night.

— —

He was Captured and Tied to a Tree.

A man with a long black cape, with a hood drawn over his head, made his appearance at Huronia and Gratiot beaches Thursday evening and frightened a number of the young ladies.

A number of young men chased the would-be Jack the Hugger, captured him, and tied him to a tree. The man later broke away and ran to the Consolidated Ice company's ice house, at Holland beach, where he was held a prisoner by the resorters until an early hour this morning. (July 25, 1908)

Well, who WAS he??? Apparently we shall never know.

Meanwhile, in a veritable crime wave, or at least prank wave, the same issue of the paper reported the following untoward event that even made the Chicago papers. The parents must've been aghast, and Huronia ablaze with gossip. Makes one wonder if the same pranksters cooked up both sprees:

YOUNG MEN ROBBED STORE
AT HURONIA BEACH DANCE HALL

— —

One Dropped Into the Arms of Policeman Enright
Late Friday Night

— —

All Pleaded Guilty and Were Fined in Police Court this Morning

— —

The Offenders Are Members of
Well-Known and Wealthy Families

— —

Four young men, residents at Huronia beach, were arrested Friday night while in the act of burglarizing the confectionery, notion, and cigar store, conducted by Burgess Bros. in connection with the Huronia beach dance hall.

For some nights past Burgess Bros. have heard noises about the place, and knowing that some pilfering had been done night after night, nailed down several of the windows. Friday

night Beach Patrolman Michael Enright decided to watch for
the offenders. About 11:15 o'clock he walked by the hall and as
he was about to turn north he saw the boys in the dance room.
Hiding at the rear in a secluded corner, he waited. A light was
turned on and then quickly extinguished. . . . Enright crept
noiselessly to the front of the building and confronted three of
the young fellows. . . . They started to run towards the cottages,
but the officer hearing a noise in the hall, ran to the window,
when to his surprise, one of the quartet fell into his arms. The
handcuffs were placed on him and Officers Fisher and Shine
were summoned.

The other three boys were by this time in bed at their respec-
tive cottages, but the officers awoke them and made them dress.
They spent the night in the police office.

This morning every effort was made to have the complaints
against the young men withdrawn, but Prosecutor Moore would
not consent. By his permission, however, they were arraigned
under fictitious names. . . . The eldest of the youths is 24 years
old, and the others are 16 to 18 years of age. All are sons of
prominent, highly respected and wealthy families. Three are
from St. Louis and one is a member of a Port Huron family
whose name has stood as the synonym of honor and integrity
for more than a generation. (July 25, 1908)

Nasty things were happening that summer of 1908:

Roy Hall, a young man residing at the beach, has made com-
plaint to the police against several young women who live at
Huronia beach. While he and a young lady friend were riding
along Gratiot avenue in an automobile the girls threw handfuls
of mud over them. (August 19, 1908)

Pranks aside, Gratiot and Huronia were not immune to serious crime, even
in the allegedly innocent years before World War I:

Some time ago thieves went through the cottages at Huronia Beach, carrying off a considerable quantity of superfluous diamonds, watches, and money. Marcus Young does not intend to have a repetition of this and has placed two night watchmen and a large mastiff on guard. (August 10, 1889)

Two weeks ago thieves entered the Windermere Hotel and some of the cottages at Huronia Beach, carrying off several pocketbooks, diamonds, and other jewelry. On Saturday last the pocketbooks were found on a stump in the woods, all right with the exception of the money. The thieves had no use for diamonds so they carefully enclosed them in the pocket books. (August 12, 1889)

FRIGHTENED THEM BADLY.

— —

A Man Attempted to Climb in the Window.

— —

At the Mitts Cottage at Gratiot Beach on Sunday Night.

— —

The Cottage Occupied by Ten Young Ladies.

— —

For some time past a number of young ladies of the city have been occupying the Mitts cottage at Gratiot beach opposite the Windermere. . . . About two o'clock Sunday morning one of the young ladies was awakened by the sound of something falling, and rising up with a start she was horrified to see a man about half way in the window. She managed to awaken some of the other girls, and then the screaming commenced and was followed immediately by the burglar's exit. There was no sleep in the Mitts' cottage for the balance of the night. (August 8, 1900)

With so many people frolicking about of a summer, accidents had to happen. There was no first-aid station around, but if you were lucky there'd be

Julia Brookes and her brother Theodore at the Port Huron train station, September 1908.

a physician on vacation who could attend to you, for example the young Dr. Theodore P. Brookes of St. Louis, fresh out of medical school:

> Really I have had more personal private practice up here during the last ten days than during the entire previous year at home. Unless I am doing better next year, it would pay me to take a cottage at Huronia and hang out my shingle for the season. To be sure, I've collected only six dollars so far but hope to get thirty more from a hospital case, and have another two due. (August 17, 1913/TPB)

There was certainly plenty of demand for a summer doctor:

> Heard calls for the doctor, so investigated. One of the younger boys had jumped from the roof of a cottage despite repeated

warnings, and broke his arm. It was a typical Pott's fracture. Dr. McKee set it very nicely as far as I could tell, but gave nothing for the twitching of the muscles except a little whiskey.

Mrs. Eyssell next door asked me to look at her daughter's face and hands. There are swollen areas on them which appear each morning with a headache, but disappear during the day. They claim to have a number of spiders and insects in the cottage and I rather think they are responsible. Gave her some "Phenol" solution to apply and advice to clear out the spiders, etc. (undated, circa 1906/TPB)

This young fellow from Detroit got mixed up with the propellor blades of a powerboat while he was bathing in the canal. As a result he narrowly escaped drowning and evisceration. I happened to be on Huronia at the time and was able to handle the case with the aid of Mother's emergency kit and mine. I had silkworm gut, catgut, needles, and my pocket case, and Mother had dressings so that I soon had him repaired. The wounds looked much worse than they really were, so my fame spread rapidly and I had two or three other patients on my hands. We soon found that cottage facilities were inadequate for a bed patient and transferred the young fellow to the hospital yesterday. (August 17, 1913/TPB)

An excited bathing-suited man washed up at the door demanding the doctor. A man had been run into by a motorboat. Fortunately, Clark had left his wheel here, so Theodore snatched up all my bandages, cotton and such like, and put in a compress, while he rode to the Farm for his instruments.

Theodore has been laughing over his professional appearance. In white duck trousers, no coat, no hat, on a wheel, and clasping one of the children's wicker suitcases for a satchel. (August 14, 1913/MPB)

Was called out of bed last night to see a gall stone colic on
Huronia. The patient was my former operating room nurse at
Female Hospital.

Collected $4.00 for two dressings of bruised fingers on Gratiot
Beach this morning. Dressed Mrs. Kidd's infected mosquito bites
last night and bandaged Dr. Riggs's swollen leg this a.m. (July
17, 1917/TPB)

Received a very urgent message from Mrs. Brokaw which effec-
tively blocked all previous engagements. To be sure there was no
great rush after all, but the patient thought there was. (August 5,
1916/TPB)

What with the cottages built of wood and heated by log fireplaces, with
primitive gas stoves in the kitchens, and oil lamps and candles in the rooms
in the early years, fire posed a major threat. Huronia had its own mini fire
department, of sorts:

A small blaze started at cottage 43 Wednesday, but was extinguished by the Huronia fire brigade. (July 9, 1904)

Other cottages—and hotels, as we have seen—were not so fortunate:

F. A. Weyers' cottage at Gratiot beach was totally destroyed by
fire on Sunday afternoon. . . . About 12:30 o'clock a member of
the family attempted to light the gasoline stove for the purpose
of preparing dinner. A quantity of gasoline caught fire, there was
an explosion, and in an instant the building was on fire. The furniture was saved but the cottage was soon reduced to ashes. . . .
An effort will be made to secure hose to keep at the beach in
case of further fires. (July 22, 1901)

Further unpleasantness involved not life and death matters, but who got to
use the beach. In 1907 Port Huron businessman Fred Hoffmann claimed he

owned the lakeshore at Huronia. Marcus Young pooh-poohed the notion, but when Mr. Hoffmann set about erecting a fence along the shore, and demanding a handsome sum of money from Mr. Young if resorters expected to set foot upon "his" beach, things got hot. The resulting tangle provided headlines that amused the reading public:

WAR DECLARED AT HURONIA BEACH (May 15, 1907)

Rumors of Shot Guns, Rifles, and Insane Men (May 16, 1907)

Fence Along Lake Shore Has Mysteriously Disappeared (May 17, 1907)

Firing of Guns and Ringing Bells Disturb Hoffman Forces (May 18, 1907)

Marcus Young Received Black Eye at Huronia Beach (May 21, 1907)

Marcus Young this morning said to *The Times*: "Fred L. Hoffman has built a fort on the lake shore. . . . Watch it disappear some night." (June 5, 1907)

The row continued into the next year, with Marcus Young arrested for trespassing and Mr. Hoffman receiving ninety days behind bars for assault. This sort of thing could not continue. Hoffman and Young settled their dispute legally, and the fence came down. Huronia owned its lakefront.

Nor was peaceful Gratiot Beach, with its privately owned cottages, immune to waterfront nastiness. Probably lot owners didn't realize their deeds didn't actually say they owned the beach in front of their cottages—just that they could use it. As later became clear, Charles Ward, the developer of Gratiot Beach, figured that in fact he still owned the lakefront sand.

In 1903 Mr. Ward sent teams to shovel up the sand so he could sell it for making concrete. The shoveling left dumbfounded Gratiot cottagers with ghastly strips of bare gravel instead of a beach, and they promptly sued.

The first court decisions sided with Mr. Ward, but on appeal the Michigan Supreme Court more commonsensically considered the cottagers' point of view, and told Mr. Ward to knock it off. Purchasers of lakefront property in Michigan, the court reasoned, shared ownership of the beach with the other lot owners, and sensibly enough, no one could use it for strip mining.[24]

Chapter 8
Bringing In the (Right) Crowds

So the crowds were flocking in, but just how did potential beachers learn of the Lake Huron resorts in the first place, in those days long before television and radio, not to mention the internet?

The most obvious means to get customers through the door was by advertising in print, and both Huronia and the Beach hotels placed ads in the Port Huron papers as well in the journals of St. Louis, Detroit, and the other large midwestern cities that traditionally supplied their clientele.

Apart from advertisements, news items about the resorts in the local and nearby papers—items probably suggested by the resort owners—also helped business, without the cost of taking out ads. No doubt Mr. Young arranged for the following story, which ran in the *Detroit Post and Tribune* in 1882 under the title "Huronia Beach" before appearing in the Port Huron paper. It's just about the earliest description of Huronia Beach we have. Of course, as basically a piece of advertising one mustn't expect unwavering accuracy in the story/ad, so just to place it all in perspective, within brackets are my own editorial comments looking back from 130 years later:

> About three miles north of Port Huron . . . Mr. Marcus Young
> of Port Huron has obtained possession of three-quarters of a
> mile of the lake shore which he has christened Huronia Beach.
> The beach here shelves off very gradually, so that for a distance
> of 200 or 300 feet or more out bathing is perfectly safe, even
> for children who cannot swim [and if you believe that, I have a
> bridge I'd like to sell you]. There is no current and there are no
> deep holes or dangerous places [never mind the undertow when
> the lake's rough]. South of this property the city of Port Huron
> owns a beautiful grove which is to be improved as a park [don't

worry, we'll keep the hoi polloi out with a fence]. From the northern limit of this, Mr. Young has established a building line for cottages, with a lawn 150 feet wide in front extending to the beach [we say "lawn," you might say sand-with-sprouts-of-grass-here-and-there]. Cottage sites are leased but not sold. Several cottages have already been built and more will be erected the coming summer.

Some of the conditions on which it is proposed to maintain the beach as a summer resort are thus stated by the proprietor:

Cottages and cottage sites are leased to parties of unexceptional character [no weirdos]. Huronia Beach differs from other resorts, from the fact that there are no accommodations provided for transient guests, picnic and excursion parties, unless entertained by owners and lessees of cottages [no riffraff either, unless they're somebody's guests].

The sale of liquors, wares or merchandise of any kind on the premises is strictly prohibited [bring your own booze for the drunken benders you have in mind]. The ambition of the proprietor is not to be ostentatious, but to conduct the place in a plain matter-of-fact way [I don't have dough for anything fancier, so don't expect the Ritz], and afford a pleasant resort where a man can bring his family into a first-class community permanently located, and at the same time "can pull off coat and boots" and enjoy a rest—and live at less expense than at home [hope you don't mind using outhouses].

Cottage sites consist of all the ground required upon which to erect a cottage. There is no limit to the size or style of building [as long as it's unexceptional]. A 12 foot space is maintained between buildings [so you'll be able to hear everything when your neighbors are on their porch], and an unobstructed view of lake in front [except for the cottages up by the chapel, which I'll have to build when the canal cuts through the property in a few years], and access to Huronia Beach grounds and appurtenances.

There is a dining hall, where cottagers and their guests are
provided with substantial food [notice I didn't say "delicious"]. . . .
If cottagers prefer they can do their own cooking [until I decide
to force everyone to eat in the dining hall, as I'll be doing in a
couple of years]. . . .

While it is our desire to lease cottage sites, we are not over
zealous to settle the beach [sounds good, not like we're des-
perate for customers at all]. Several applications for sites have
been rejected [don't ask too closely how many, and why]. We
do not inquire as to an applicant's financial standing, but must
be informed as to social standing, and have confidence that
those having cottages and those who may hereafter locate, will
refuse to recommend any person to lease cottage or site not in
harmony with the requirements of the place [no axe murderers
please, otherwise ok]. We feel assured that all those holding
leases will appreciate the position taken, and assist in keeping
up the present excellent social standing of the society at Huronia
Beach. (April 28, 1882)

That last line raises the question, Whom should the new holiday spot seek
to attract? After all, resorts might direct their marketing to any angle on the
wide arc of human society: the debauched or the debonair, the tippler or
the teetotaler, the vamp or the virtuous. Each type offered a way to turn a
profit, but one couldn't mix them together and expect to win satisfied, re-
peat customers. So management had to pick its targeted clientele.

Having proven so immediately popular with the summer bathing crowd
thronging in from town, Huronia seemed at first to teeter between the social
extremes as the *Port Huron Daily Times* of August 8, 1881, informs us, with
a wink, that cottagers complained ". . . of the too free exhibitions of 'the
human form divine' which this popularity brings." But we know that the
Baptist Sunday School also picnicked at the lake in these early years. Making
his choice, early on Mr. Young aimed his marketing at the more decorous

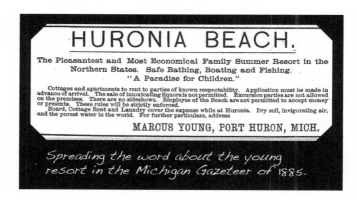

Spreading the word about the young resort in the Michigan Gazeteer of 1885.

(and more stable and moneyed) end of the social spectrum now flocking to the country's vacation spots. And so the keyword at Huronia, as at America's middle-class family resorts generally, became *respectability*—whatever that might mean exactly—along with the soupçon of exclusivity the term implied. Respectability seemed somehow to involve children, or those who didn't mind children around:

> The universal testimony of those who have spent portions of the
> summer months at Huronia and Gratiot is that the beach resorts
> are especially delightful and healthful for young children, while
> all can find both rest and recreation there. (September 2, 1889)

So Huronia sought the right sort of people and their children, yes, but steered clear of creating an *haut monde* by the lake. As the brochure of 1884 plainly declared, "The children's mothers want rest from fashion and society." The clientele might fit right in with the upper crust at home, but perfectly proper Mother and Dad could kick off their shoes at Lake Huron.

> This quiet place would afford little pleasure to a city belle with a
> Saratoga full of new dresses calculated to "astonish the natives,"
> or to the "howling swell" who would faint at the idea of being
> seen in his shirt sleeves, and who wouldn't handle an oar for
> fear of blistered and browned hands, but those who love nature,

Accepted into Huronia: the Dr. H. S. Brookes family of St. Louis. Theodore, Elizabeth, Jean, Julia, Louise, Katharine, H. S., Harry, and Mary on the beach in 1910.

> who want quiet, with yet a sense of human companionship,
> who can forego gossip and scandal, and be happy in simple
> pleasures, can find here rare delight in sea and sky and shore.
> (August 22, 1882/MF)

Woe to townsfolk who thought they might rub elbows with the Huronia out-of-towners:

> There are no accommodations for "transients," picnic and excur-
> sion parties are not allowed to fling pickle ends and watermelon
> rinds over the lawns, being in fact debarred from trespassing.
> (August 15, 1882/MF)

So there, Port Huron. This was a private resort, no public playground. And in future Mr. Young kept Huronia exclusive—a gated community of its day:

> Geo. Woodward and Geo. Chamberlain, of Fort Gratiot, were
> arrested and brought before Justice Robeson on Wednesday for
> trespassing on Huronia Beach. Both were fined. Huronia Beach is
> private property. . . . The occupants of cottages are strangers and
> claim to have no interest in the general public. (August 4, 1892)

Throughout its existence Huronia continued to practice exclusivity when it came to admitting new cottagers, or at least so management claimed. We don't know the screening procedure, if there really was one, but in his advertising Mr. Young claimed that screening of applicants served as the key to his resort's success, since it meant his customers could be sure that only persons of their same social and economic status would share their vacation haven.

> Huronia Beach is a resort peculiar in itself. . . . Mr. Young's plan
> is to furnish a quiet and safe place. . . . The general public finds
> no admission to this place and no families are accepted as ten-
> ants unless they be known in some way to the proprietor. By this
> policy the society at Huronia is of the best. (May 4, 1901)

Ads from 1911, in the golden era of the resort's popularity, invoked the camping craze that had swept the country by then. As at a well-supervised camp, parents could spend summer in a pretty spot where they wouldn't have to worry what the kids were up to.

> Huronia Beach Camp
> The children's paradise—No signs to "Keep off the Grass" at Huro-
> nia. No tired mothers at Huronia when the sun goes down. . . .
> No dressing family for meals—A sensible solution of what consti-
> tutes rest and recreation by a sensible class of people. (August 26,
> 1911)

Mr. Young's efforts to cultivate a safe and exclusive atmosphere at Huronia paid off so handsomely that in later years some families with the wherewithal to do so sent their children on ahead, under the tutelage of a family retainer.

> The Judson children and maid have arrived and are occupying
> cottage 35. Mr. and Mrs. Judson will come later. (June 29, 1916)

In news items that praised the resorts, the local papers acknowledged the obvious: what was good for Beach was good for Town, since summer visitors kept the city's cash registers ringing:

> A city merchant informs us that some of his best customers are
> the Huronia Beach cottagers. These people leave a good many
> thousand dollars in the city during the season. (August 6, 1888)

Pretty soon the resorters were helping out the town by doing the advertising themselves:

> Dr. Riggs, of Cincinnati: "The people of Port Huron are fortunate
> indeed. The members of my family have done a great amount
> of shopping in the city during their stay here—and they are not
> novices in the business—and we find that in very many lines, es-
> pecially in dry goods, prices are much lower than in Cincinnati."
> (August 31, 1895)

The town paper aimed to convince readers why Port Huron was the happening place in summer:

> For nearly a quarter century *The Times* has boomed this city and
> contiguous territory as the most delightful summer resort in
> Michigan, lacking the hot days of the more southerly places and
> the very cold days which occasionally prevail at Mackinac and
> other north Michigan resorts . . . The great panorama of passing
> marine is nowhere else to be seen on this earth. (May 4, 1901)

Sometimes the snow-weary locals had to smile at what attracted resorters:

> Port Huron people marvel at the way the beach people enjoy
> the cool weather. It has been a record breaker this year for cool

weather and yet when north winds blew strongest the resorters
seemed most to enjoy themselves, especially those who came
from interior cities where the heat is usually intense. It is the cool
weather that attracts them. . . . The fame of Port Huron seems to
be spreading. (September 5, 1903)

Now and again the transportation companies serving Port Huron gave resorts a bit of free advertising, since increased business benefited both. The
D&C steamer line's novella of 1895, *Three on a Tour*, tempted travelers to
book trips (on company ships, of course) to the pretty resorts they sailed past
aboard D&C vessels, in this case Huronia and Gratiot Beach:

Shortly after leaving Port Huron . . . as we put out into Lake Huron Mr. Harts called our attention to a beautiful beach that ran
down to the water's edge. A little farther up we saw twin villages
nestling upon the sands. They were long rows of cottages, built
around what seemed a central hall.

"Notice those two places," said Mr. Harts. "They are famous
family resorts."

"But how oddly they are built!" said Nett.

"The cottages are only lodgings, and the large central building is a dining hall where all are supplied with meals."[25]

Not to be outdone, the rival White Star line of steamers between Detroit and
Port Huron subtly plugged the lakeshore in its *White Star Magazine* of 1918:

There's the most delicious hour or two of rest while the boat lies
at the wharf at Port Huron. "Uncle" had a nap. Patricia and the
boys took a run out to beautiful Gratiot Beach on the trolley. . . .[26]

Meanwhile, on land, the Grand Trunk Railway, the main line that counted
on summer traffic into Port Huron for a goodly share of its profits in eastern
Michigan, also jumped in to help promote the town and its beach resorts.
It sounds as though the Grand Trunk's publicity staff had been reading Mr.
Young's brochures:

> When the tourist reaches Port Huron, he finds everything for
> which heart could wish. . . . Electric cars are the means of
> communication to the beaches and summer cottages north of
> town . . . where the music of the restless waves makes ceaseless
> harmony by day and night. (May 24, 1907)

Printed ads and stories helped spread the word, yes, but despite it all, most
resorters came because someone whose opinion they trusted recommended
it. After all, the best advertising, then as now, is word of mouth. One prime
source for trusted opinions was fellow churchgoers:

> We have quite a church crowd this year, the Sloans, Fishers,
> Chapmans, and ourselves from our church, and quite a number
> from other churches. (July 23, 1905/TPB)

Some newspaper clips read like personal recommendations from friends:

> "Why," said Mr. Chase [of Strathroy, Ontario], "one may travel, I
> might say, the entire length of Canada, and not be able to find
> a spot so well suited for health, rest, and recreation as these
> beaches. . . . This is my first visit to this locality, but you can say
> in the Times that it will not be my last." (August 5, 1892)

> "People are not going to the seashore as formerly," said Mr.
> Rowley. "They are beginning to find that your inland lake, with
> its miles of sandy shore, is preferable to the crowded resorts of
> the eastern and western watering places, and we have nothing
> near our home, which is at Cleveland, O., to compare with your
> vast advantages in the gifts of nature." (August 29, 1892)

> "A vacation for us without Port Huron included is like an unfin-
> ished story—very flat," said Emerson J. Schofield, who with Mrs.
> Schofield has been a steady summer visitor at Keewahdin and
> Gratiot beaches for more than 30 years. (August 27, 1939)

With the advent of the resorts, alongside the ads a new feature began to appear in the Port Huron newspapers: the summer society column. As early as 1882, only three years after Huronia came to life, the local newspapers began asking resorters Who Was Summering at Which Beach, and With Whom.

And so the summer beach column was born. What may seem but a simple gossip column at first glance in fact served several purposes. Not least among them, seeing one's name in the columns let beachers know who was where and what was up, building anticipation at seeing old friends or meeting new ones, and setting minds to potential matchmaking. The columns also helped resort owners, thanks to a virtually free form of advertising that flattered the customers who saw their names in print, subtly encouraging them to come back next year for more royal treatment.

For their part, the newspapers smiled on the columns because putting resorters' names in print helped sell the paper to these out-of-towners, who otherwise might not bother forking over the price of the local rag. Townies also read the columns because local families owned or rented cottages at the lake too, but even readers whose family had no connection to the beach might enjoy the summer hijinks of the smart set there. In short, the columns offered something for nearly everyone.

Back in the resorters' hometowns the same phenomenon occurred in reverse, as society columns in small- and large-town newspapers across the Midwest—certainly in St. Louis, and as far afield as Dallas—announced how the So-and-so's would be spending their summer at Huronia Beach or Gratiot Beach, Michigan, among the other watering places listed.

Typically once a week throughout summer, the Port Huron papers' beach columns duly dropped names and chronicled events. Huronia resorters, for example, would want to know that:

> Mr. E. B. Taylor's family have taken Mr. Wm. Stocking's cottage at Huronia Beach for the next two weeks, after which Mr. Stocking, who is managing editor of the Detroit Post and Tribune, will find it convenient to occupy it himself with his family. (July 15, 1882)

Last night Judge Vance illuminated the beach with the light of his countenance. (July 11, 1894)

Major G. M. Abbott, of Covington, Ky., who with his family is occupying a cottage at Huronia, won his title in the Mexican war. He graduated from West Point and formerly lived as a neighbor to General Grant in St. Louis, with whom he was an intimate acquaintance. (July 23, 1898)

Mrs. Wm. Reid and family, from Detroit, arrived at Huronia on Friday. Mrs. Reid was one of the earliest cottagers at Huronia. (August 6, 1898)

Mr. and Mrs. W. D. Daly, of Toledo, are visitors at the Smith cottage at Huronia. The Daly family has been at the Beaches for a number of years and has a long list of friends among the pioneer residents. (August 13, 1898)

P. J. Neff, of Cincinnati, has begun his 12th season at Huronia and is with his family at cottage 60 at the extreme north. Mr. Neff has the honor of having been president of the Cincinnati College of Music for ten years and is still a member of the board of trustees. He is one of the gentlemen at the beach whom it is a pleasure to meet during the season. (June 24, 1899)

While Gratiot and the Windermere folk would thrill to learn that:

The charming cottage of Mr. Lindenberg, south of the Windermere, has been much improved by the filling in and sodding of the grounds around it. (August 17, 1895)

A delightful dancing party was given at the Cram cottage for some of the young people at Gratiot Beach Thursday night. The house was prettily decorated with Chinese lanterns. (August 17, 1895)

J. W. Jenks, professor of political economy in Cornell university, with his family, arrived at the Windermere on Friday evening and will remain for the summer. (July 3, 1897)

Mrs. Wm. G. Caldwell and Miss Caldwell, of Cincinnati, who are at the Windermere, are among the former patrons of that resort for many years. They have good reason to love the breezes of Lake Huron. (August 13, 1898)

Passenger Agent Crane, of the Wabash railroad, with his family from St. Louis, are expected at their Gratiot cottage today. (June 16, 1900)

Henry I. Armstrong is giving his Gratiot cottage a thorough repainting. (May 25, 1901)

Mrs. H. D. Crane, a Cincinnatian, who is in love with the climate and pleasures of Gratiot, has arrived at the Windermere on her annual visit. (July 19, 1902)

John Siebert is building an automobile house back of his Gratiot beach cottage. (July 9, 1904)

Mr. and Mrs. Williston P. Munger and family, of Kansas City, are occupying a cottage at Gratiot beach for the summer and are taking their meals at the Windermere. (July 4, 1919)

When St. Louis, Mo., begins to turn on its famous sultry weather,
the R. E. Holekamps and Mrs. L. C. Hermann start their annual
trek to Gratiot beach for cool dips in Lake Huron and restful
sunbaths on the sand. (August 1, 1943)

Town girls could see these summer arrivals as unwelcome competition:

And now that we're up to the beach every day this weather, we
have time to renew acquaintance with our delightful summer
residents. There was a time some years ago when we actually
dreaded the arrival of these families with their attractive young
daughters—all the town boys thought they were terribly smart if
they had a beach girl to date during the summer months! And
were we happy when Labor Day came along and the general
exodus from the beaches began. But don't let it worry you, girls,
the boys married us after all! (July 10, 1938)

Well, not always, as the St. Louis newspaper tells us:

From Gratiot Beach, Port Huron, Mich., comes the announce-
ment of the engagement of Miss Arline Clark, daughter of Mr.
and Mrs. Cyrus E. Clark, to John N. Lassen of Port Huron. Mr.
and Mrs. Clark are among the St. Louisans who have a cottage at
"Gratiot," and have gone there every summer for several years.
(September 6, 1915/SLPD)

Through the years the beach column took different names: "Around the
Beaches" (1894, this date being when the name made its first appearance),
"At the Beaches" (1895), "Lake Huron Breezes" (1898), "Life Giving Breezes" (1898), "On Lake Huron's Shore" (1899), "Breezes from the Beaches"
(1899), "Along the Beaches" (1900), "In Cool Breezes" (1900), "Gratiot
Beach" (1900), "Gossip from the Beaches" (1900), "Gaities of Vacation Time"
(1901), and "The Very Idea" (1937).

Homespun artwork for the Beach Society column. August 1895 (right) and July 1899 (below).

By the 1930s, with Huronia gone and Gratiot now an "old" resort with history behind it, society columns reflected the hierarchy that ranked you according to when your family first came to the beach:

> Mrs. William H. Taylor, who has been a beach resident here
> for 52 years, entertained old residents at Gratiot beach at an
> afternoon tea Wednesday in her summer home. She and the late
> Dr. Taylor, and the family of the late John Siebert, all of Cincin-
> nati, were the first summer residents to come to Gratiot beach.
> Daughters of John Siebert who attended the party are Mrs. Frank
> DuPuy, Mrs. E. J. Scarlet, and Miss Annie Mae Siebert, all of
> Cincinnati. Miss Mary Alice Finney, daughter of the late Judge
> Finney, Detroit, whose family started coming to the beach a few
> years later than the two original families, was present. Mrs. W.
> S. Greene, sister of the late Dr. Riggs, an early arrival, and Dr.

Calling it like it is: the Beach column headliner, August 24, 1907.

Riggs's daughters, Mrs. R. M. Atkins and Mrs. T. P. Brookes, now summer residents at the beach, were among the guests at the party, who numbered about 30. Mrs. Earl Galbraith, daughter of Peter Rudolph Neff, also an early resident here, and Mrs. Alfred G. Allen, both of Cincinnati, who are at Gratiot Inn, attended. Mrs. Taylor's daughter, Mrs. August Marx, Cincinnati, her guest, assisted her. (August 6, 1936; never mind that the reporter flubbed the genealogy—Mrs. Greene and Mrs. Brookes were niece and grandniece of Dr. Riggs, not sister and daughter—the point was these folks and the others figured as Gratiot blue-bloods by virtue of sheer longevity.)

The beach columns soldiered on through World War II but died away in the early 1950s, as the ongoing conversion of cottages into year-round residences left the summer colony too meager for roving reporters to mine. Thereafter any news of beach residents could easily fit into the town society column—itself a dying breed, as social reporting of personal doings began to seem passé. Society had changed, and with it, newspaper reporting.

Nowadays perhaps no one would dream of advertising to would-be burglars their absentia from winter homes. Even in the allegedly bucolic 1890s, resorters could recoil at the thought:

A lady patron was approached Thursday by a *Times* reporter.
When she was told the occasion of the visit she at once refused

to be interviewed. "Do you object to having your name appear in print?" asked the reporter.

"Most certainly I do," the lady replied.

"Why?" asked the reporter.

"Well, I will tell you. Not a few people are aware of the fact that in all large cities there are organized bands of burglars and marauders who watch the columns of the public press. Perhaps they find out that Mrs. Jones, of 215 Eighth street, Chicago, has gone to a summer resort to spend three or four months. Of course it looks like a harmless little expression, but it means a lot to the people who are in the safe-cracking and house-breaking business. The house is broken open during the absence of the people at the beaches. The burglar succeeds in getting everything except the cooking stove and the baby carriage. If this was traced down to the bottom I believe you would find out this same, harmless little newspaper item did the work. This may appear strange, but nevertheless I believe it." (August 5, 1892)

That reader's disquiet notwithstanding, in its heyday summer beach gossip formed a major component of Port Huron's journalistic *oeuvre*, with kid reporters roving from cottage to cottage to beg, "Any news?"

Chapter 9
Getting There, Leaving There

In terms of sheer excitement, nothing all year, except maybe Christmas Eve, compared to Port Huron Night—the night before my family would leave home in St. Louis to drive to Michigan. My parents, especially Mom, had been busy for days getting everything and everyone ready, but being a kid I basically just had to show up with everyone else in the car bright and early that hallowed morning when we headed for the lake, 630 miles from home.

In the 1950s, the drive to Michigan meant one highway above all: Route 66. With Dad at the wheel of the 1955 Ford station wagon, the trip started with a highlight, the thrilling ride past downtown St. Louis skyscrapers and over the broad and placid Mississippi. Highlight over, we settled in for the long journey through the seemingly endless cornfields of Illinois, toward Chicago.

Mom had made tuna sandwiches and filled the green-and-white thermos jug to the top with sugary lemonade. She'd picked up comic books to amuse us kids, but the rule was we couldn't open them before Springfield, Illinois, in order to make them last, and that was 100 miles away, a good two hours. Meanwhile we'd play word games and Spot-the-Farthest-License-Plate. We'd also sing, my father, with his rich baritone, leading us in *Meet Me in St. Louie, Louie*, which stoked our civic pride, *Glory, Glory Hallelujah*, which stoked our national pride, and *Bill Grogan's Goat*, which was vaguely disconcerting because it involved tying a goat to railroad tracks, though everything came out okay for the goat in the end. Between parental efforts to distract us, I'd help our cocker spaniel Minerva stick her nose out the window (no air conditioning then), watch the Ford's speedometer (a nifty red arrow that glowed at night), and wonder aloud how much longer till we got out of Illinois. The latter was an inherited trait, since my grandmother Agnes, when particularly provoked along the same route, would let out a heartfelt "Illinois drivers—durn their buttons!", the closest she would ever come to cussing.

In later years Mom would retell the story of "Sunrise in Toledo." On the annual northerly trek the summer I was still a babe in arms, the last of the brood of four kids, my parents decided to stay the night in northern Indiana, the six of us (seven, counting Minerva the dog, which we certainly did) in one hotel room. All went well until I started crying during the night, Mom said, and repeatedly so. Every time Dad got up to tend me he'd hit his head on the shelf over the headboard of my parents' bed, just like in a television skit. Then some hours later Mom awoke to an unpleasant dampness, because my three-year-old sister, who for some reason had wanted to sleep between Mom and Dad, had wet the bed. Dad got up to get towels, hitting his head again, and as he staggered wearily toward the bathroom he slid into a split, where Minerva had left an unfortunate solid deposit on the carpet. That's when Mom called it quits, getting us up at 4:00 in the morning with the creative ruse that we were going to see the legendary sunrise in Toledo.

But all that was long after the advent of the Automobile Age around 1910 or so, when progressively better cars and roads meant vacationers could drive to Lake Huron. Before then, public transit was the traveler's only option, unless you were wealthy enough to own a private railway car. Public transit meant your choice of steamship or train in the earliest years of the resorts, augmented by the interurban trolley from Detroit once that line debuted in 1900, or finally a bus, after Gratiot Avenue was paved through between Port Huron and Detroit in 1919.[27]

Trains from Detroit, along the Grand Trunk Railway, had called since 1858 at the Fort Gratiot Depot just north of Port Huron. That wooden building still stands, a museum nowadays under the Blue Water Bridge, thanks to its role in Thomas Edison's boyhood. Some thirty years later, trains from Chicago and points south began calling at the ornate new Grand Trunk station once it opened in the southwest end of town, in 1891.

Huronia and Gratiot resorters formed a large chunk of passenger traffic at the Grand Trunk station:

> A company of St. Louis people reached the beaches this morn-
> ing, coming by special car from that city by way of the C. & G.
> T. Twenty-three families from St. Louis will spend the summer at
> the resorts. (June 24, 1899)

In St. Louis's heyday as Queen of the Lake Huron beaches, St. Louis newspapers sported ads from the railroads in competition for the lucrative summer
passenger traffic to Michigan. By 1904, both the Wabash and the Illinois
Central lines heralded to the St. Louis reading public their "two through
sleeping cars to Huronia Beach." That meant you didn't have to change
trains in Chicago; your sleeping car was uncoupled and attached to a Port
Huron–bound train while you slept. Ohioans and others farther east didn't
have the through-to-Port-Huron service, but they did have the overnight
Lake Erie boats and frequent trains into and out of the rising metropolis of
Detroit.

Seems the Wabash Railroad had a reputation, and not for through
sleeping cars:

> I shall leave Detroit at 6pm Wednesday, reaching St. Louis at
> 7:58am Thursday, provided the Wabash surprises itself and gets
> in on time. The agent in Detroit declares the trains have been
> running close to schedule of late, but I can't but doubt such
> news. (August 17, 1913/TPB)

> For the first time in its life the Wabash train got in on time in De-
> troit. The Prewitts came up on the same train with us. They have
> Cottage 24. We got in in time for dinner. Our trunks didn't come,
> so we could idle about all afternoon. I'd just as soon be back in
> St. Louis, though, as it is decidedly cool. (June 12, 1914/JIB)

By 1909 the rival Alton Railroad touted itself as "the Only Way" from St.
Louis to Wisconsin and Michigan, specifically noting "Detroit—Port Huron—
Huronia Beach Camp" in its St. Louis advertising. Mentioning Huronia Beach

Agnes Greene at the Port Huron train station, 1910.

but oddly forgetting Lake Huron, one ad crooned to sweltering St. Louisans how "the cool waters of Lakes Michigan, Ontario, and Erie just yearn for you." (August 1, 1910/SLPD)

Not missing your train to the Beach could require crafty maneuvering, especially if you were a physician:

> Harry says he has found why Dad never told patients when
> he was leaving for vacation. I have found it wise to date the
> vacation at least one or two days prior to actually leaving town.
> That gives a few hours to pack and to see the last few cases that

should be seen before getting away. Patients and casual visitors
just will wait until the last hours prior to train time for their
farewell visits. (July 31, 1945/TPB)

Travel by train might be comfy but wasn't exactly swift by today's standards,
and it kept you on your toes:

> I have bought my ticket and made my reservation, leaving here
> [St. Louis] Monday on the 11:52 P.M. train to Chicago. I plan
> to leave Chicago 11:25 P.M. Tuesday, arriving in Detroit at 7:25
> A.M. Wednesday, all by Wabash. That is Central time, of course.
> I ought to be able to get the Interurban leaving Detroit at 10:10
> A.M. Eastern time, and getting into Port Huron at 12:50 P.M.
> (July 15, 1922/TPB)

Changing trains could elevate the blood pressure:

> We had just 1½ hours between trains in Chicago and had to
> make the ride from the Dearborn St. station to the Union Depot.
> The train left Port Huron 1 hour and 20 minutes late and was
> still an hour late at 6 a.m. There went our train connection,
> meaning a wait with one small and impatient boy of 8 months
> in a hot station for 3 hours. But the fireman shoveled more coal
> into the firebox of the engine, redcaps appeared most unexpect-
> edly, the cab director whistled up a dashing taxi and we boarded
> the panting C&A train with a full two minutes to spare! (August
> 15, 1943/TPB)

The delight of sleeping on the train might not be what it was cracked up to be:

> For comfort and convenience I occupied a Drawing Room from
> Port Huron to Chicago. The comfort was not all that one would
> like. The berth was right over the trucks of the car. All eight
> wheels on that truck seemed to be on their own route, leaping
> forward, jumping upward and rolling sideways from tie to tie or

> rail to rail. If only they had synchronized their gyrations it would
> not have been so bad. Two nights later, in a bedroom on the
> Alton I had both comfort and convenience, sleeping soundly.
> (September 10, 1944/TPB)

If your train (or Lake Erie steamer) from home landed you in Detroit you could hop a motor-driven interurban electric rail car on up to Port Huron, after the line opened in August 1900. That ride took some two and one-quarter to three and one-half hours (as opposed to today's one hour by car), which still gave you enough time to get out from town and open up your cottage on the lake.

> Detroit and Gratiot. Rain towards morning, but none while we
> were in Detroit. Landed at 6, breakfasted uptown, took 9 A.M.
> special trolley, reached Port Huron 11:15, lunched, bought
> supplies & came to cottage. Found evidence of someone having
> entered it, nothing missing. Took off a few shutters, swept out.
> Fine here. Carried water from Dr. Holdom next door, who has
> been on the Beach 10 days. Electric light turned on in cottage.
> (May 10, 1911/ADGdiary)

You had to be careful about time, in those days before standardization of daylight saving time:

> Went at once to Interurban station . . . found we had missed 9:15
> trolley on which we hoped to meet Clark, as we did not know
> Detroit had changed to Eastern time. (May 21, 1915/ADGdiary)

After the roads improved, beginning in 1922 a prosaic bus would do from Detroit. You just had to mind your schedules:

> Celia left her at the Wabash Station after 6 o'clock to take the
> 7:05 bus to Port Huron, as the next one would not get her here
> till nearly midnight, with no way to get out to the Beach. (Au-
> gust 22, 1929/ADG)

And you'd have to deal with crowds, especially during World War II when gasoline rationing meant public transit was packed:

> The R.D.B. contingent arrived Thursday, Bob standing on the bus
> all the way from Detroit. (August 13, 1944/TPB)

Hardy (foolhardy?) souls could forsake the comfort of a railway compartment, though, for that new form of transportation, the automobile, once it came on the scene in large-ish numbers after 1910 or so. At least it was private transportation:

> At Huronia Beach . . . Mr. Waite and family, of Little Rock,
> Arkansas, made the entire trip by automobile, in nine and one-
> half days, averaging about 150 miles per day. Mr. Waite stated
> that the worst stretch of road he encountered on the entire trip
> was between Mt. Clemens and Port Huron. (June 25, 1915; that
> "worst stretch" being the last forty miles of the trip)

Early automobile travel required careful reading of maps and route books, in those days before road signs guided auto drivers. Here's how the Cincin-

Agnes Brookes and her 1939 Oldsmobile, just home from church, 1940.

nati Automobile Club's *Official Blue Book* of 1916, taken along by Agnes's cousins from Ohio, directed motorists to drive out of downtown Port Huron that year (numbers indicating mileage):

> Go south with trolley on Military St., running over railroad at
> 1.0; straight ahead where trolley leaves, 2.1, running along
> shore of St. Clair River. Cross railroad switch at 2.8, picking up
> trolley at 3.1; cross trolley and railroad at 3.8. Fork at 3.9; bear
> left along railroad, passing salt works (on left—4.3). Swing left
> with road across trolley at 4.6; straight ahead along shore of
> river with some beautiful views of same.[28]

And that only put you some four miles out of town! Still, more and more folks risked the roads in a "machine" so they wouldn't have to share their journey with strangers on a train:

> You will be surprised to see the number of machines on the
> beaches. Evidently the automobile thief is unknown in this part
> of the country, for they are left alongside the road all night or
> just backed into the yards of the cottages. I have noticed two
> from St. Louis, one a Dorris of the vintage of 1913. (August 17,
> 1913/TPB)

Premature optimism, it turned out, as the following summer the Port Huron paper warned "Auto Thieves Are Busy at Beaches" (September 5, 1914).

The motorcar became more of an option once roads improved in the 1920s. In fact the better roads and improved cars meant folks could reasonably drive from farther afield. That included St. Louis—but as Agnes reported, not without drawbacks one didn't face on the train:

> As you see we made Detroit but it was a touch and go affair for
> a while, for it has poured steadily almost all day. We stopped,
> as I wrote last night, at Chicago Heights. Never again for me, if
> I can help it. The service was so slow and <u>so</u> poor, the place so

noisy and even the water wouldn't run out of the tub without a lot of coaxing. I was glad to leave. I got up about five and we had left by six—didn't try to get breakfast there but waited until nearly eight and had a nice breakfast at a small town near.

We had a blowout this morning. It happened on a very lonely stretch of road, in the middle of nowhere, in the midst of one of our worst downpours. I just sat still, not wishing to get out in all that deluge. Finally it slackened somewhat so I got out, got the jack out and began operations. Just as I was adjusting the jack a truck came along and asked if I wanted help. I accepted with pleasure and he put it on in just a few minutes. I gave him fifty cents and we went our way rejoicing.

When we reached Elkhart [Indiana] I tried to have the tire repaired but the boy came back to tell me that there was a long gash in it and that it would have to be vulcanized, which would take two or three days and then might not hold. He sold me a new Dunlop tire for $11.85, having allowed me $6.00 on the old tire. Only after we were miles away did I remember that you did not care for a Dunlop tire. I'm sorry but I was afraid to risk that long a haul without a spare so I took what seemed good at the time. (June 20, 1927/AGB, written on stationery of Hotel Statler, Detroit)

But the most scenic route between Port Huron and Detroit—and the most fun to a kid's way of thinking—was also the oldest: by steamship, along the St. Clair River. Regular river service dated back to 1829, but by the heyday of Port Huron's resorts after 1890, just two great rivals competed for resorters' business: the D&C Line and the White Star Line, with the White Star Line commanding the lion's share of the trade.[29]

Between May and November the White Star's *City of Toledo* plied the river, a familiar sight after the ship entered service in 1896.

The steamer *City of Toledo* was put on the river route last week, which is always a harbinger of the resort season. (May 18, 1901)

Side-wheel steamers *Tashmoo* and *City of Alpena* catering
to the summer trade at Port Huron. Postcard, 1908.

Going back home at the end of the season, you'd take the steamer too, if
you could. The trip took longer than the interurban or train to Detroit, but
something about being on a ship was just plain more fun.

> Father expects to come up for the last few days so as to help us
> close, and then we all expect to go down to Detroit together. We
> are planning to take the D&C. Our railroad ticket is interchange-
> able on the D&C lines, and that will be a pleasanter trip. We
> leave here at 9:45 and reach Detroit at 1:35, if on time. (Sep-
> tember 18, 1917/AGB)

For many, the steamer of choice between Port Huron and Detroit, after she
entered service in 1900, was the White Star Line's unforgettable *Tashmoo*.
From her debut in 1900 until her untimely demise after grounding in 1936,
the gleaming white side-wheeler, belching coal smoke from her twin stacks,
sped up and down the St. Clair River with room for 2,500 passengers to
enjoy the view.

Left: The steamer Tash-moo approaches Port Huron, 1930. Below: Ella and Dick Atkins of Cincinnati savor the St. Clair River to Gratiot Beach, 1929.

Whether one traveled by train, steamer, interurban, or automobile, re-sorters with enough time and money to stay for weeks or months shipped trunks ahead from home, via the railroads. Picking them up at Port Huron's train station, the city's street railway transported the trunks out to the Beaches.

The big excursion car of the streetcar line was in commission on Friday handling baggage for people coming to Gratiot and Huronia. (June 16, 1900)

When the sad time came to leave for home, trunks headed back to the station by means of the same conveyance, before their owners left the Beach:

> The street railway's baggage car is in active commission in these days, transporting the luggage of home-seekers from Gratiot and Huronia. (August 31, 1897)

> My trunk went at seven this morning so I hope I will see it on time tomorrow. (September 8, 1914/JIB)

> A big express package arrived from Port Huron two days ago. Today a huge trunk appeared. Sort of looks like the chap who threw in his hat first to see whether or not he dared to go home. So I guess my wife meant it when she told me over the phone Friday that she will be home early Tuesday morning. (September 24, 1944/TPB)

Your ship or train or trolley or bus landed you in Port Huron. Now how did you cover the last four-plus miles, out to the beaches north of town?

At the beginning of the resorts, in 1880, Mr. Young had his horse-drawn omnibus to Huronia, yet the dirt road leading north from Port Huron was nothing to write home about. More like a dust alley, or mud swamp if it rained. But the city had opened Lakeside Cemetery up that way, and in the nineteenth century cemetery visiting was the Sunday fashion, so in June 1882 Port Huron joined with the neighboring village of Fort Gratiot to cooperate in "putting the road leading to Lakeside Cemetery in good order," as the *Times* trumpeted. Whatever that meant exactly—probably laying down gravel—Huronia Beach would benefit from it too since the resort lay right across the road from the graveyard.

Only four years later, in 1886, the city surveyed the route with an eye to introducing electric trolleys between Fort Gratiot and Huronia Beach. Remarkably early this, and indeed Port Huron became the second city in the

United States to install an electric trolley system that survived.[30] The trolleys supplemented the "new gravel road" out to the lake, and offered quicker transit between the Beaches and town, especially to the steamers with their fast riverine service to and from Detroit.

Port Huron's Electric Railway trolleys were open-air when introduced (must've been bracing in chilly weather), with seats whose backs could be reversed for the return trip into town. The four and one-quarter mile trip from Black River in downtown Port Huron out to the Windermere Hotel took some twenty minutes. It certainly beat horse-drawn carriages.

Above: Behind Gratiot cottages in 1915, nothing but the dirt road and street-car tracks leading into town. Left: Streetcar and paved road, 1925.

Up North

Steamers to and from Detroit tied up at the foot of Port Huron's Grand River Avenue, so you still had to hie yourself over the four blocks between the dock and Huron Avenue, where the trolley cars ran:

> If there is no one to carry our bags up Grand River, we can take
> a taxi to the streetcar. (August 5, 1926/AGB)

In 1987 my father, aged seventy-four at the time, put down on paper his memories of journeying to Gratiot Beach from St. Louis by train, steamer, and trolley, as a lad in the early 1920s with his mother, Agnes, four siblings, and the housekeeper, Celia:

Up North

Sometime in February the process began. To us, the passive
beneficiaries, there was enchantment, a mounting rapture not
fully achieved until we had in fact been transported "Up North."
I cannot say what was the first sign that set our clocks, started
our little humming motors. A word, a reminiscence? Maybe it
was after the Christmas trappings had all been put away, and the
household was settling into the humdrum. Possibly it was a slight
lifting of our Mother's spirits—for she was highly complicitous. I
don't know if there were negotiations with Grandmother. I doubt
it; I think Grandmother Greene had become resigned that we
five and her only daughter would come whooping up to the cottage, our importunities the reality, her afternoon nap a fantasy.
  There was a sense that Going Up North for the summer (for
this is what it came to—every last hour from the end of school
to the reopening was contrived to be spent at the Lake) was
required for Mother's health. It was a compensation for having
had five children in five and a half years, and she should not
have to spend the summer in the heat of St. Louis. There was no
argument from us about that.
  We argued about everything else, however. Grandmother
would try to straighten us out when we became too obnox-

ious, but generally she left discipline, management, ordering food, planning meals to the established pattern of our family. As it were, she was a guest in her own house, her prerogatives sketchily defined in injunctions against slamming doors, against talking loudly during her nap-time between 1 and 2pm (we were supposed to be digesting our noon meal anyway, spending a quiet hour before the afternoon swim).

We knew we were privileged. It had to be so—anything so much fun must be envied. To be sure, our friends thought it was dumb for us to cut out just when things were getting good at home, what with school out.

There were clear signals as to the imminence of our Going Up North. Signals other than school drawing to a close. Mother was putting things aside and then leaning over a cavernous trunk supplemented by two steamer trunks. One day they would be gone, spirited off by the St. Louis Transfer Company while we were at school, and not to be seen again till we had arrived at the cottage. Nor were the trunks of concern to us so long as our swimming gear could be gotten at quickly. Even that was of no great concern. If the trunks were not at hand that very first afternoon, there were old suits of another era we were not ashamed to don. The "mustard suit" served generations of males, even when its little skirt was grotesquely out of style.

We were driven to St. Louis Union Station in the touring car and herded aboard the Wabash sleeping car. "Herded" is incorrect: we had to be restrained. We were assigned our berths, which were already made up. We fought for the upper berth, but it made no difference. I suppose it was settled on an alternating-years basis. My sister slept on the divan bed in the Drawing Room, leaving Mother with the baby on the bottom bunk . . . and that leaves two people unaccounted for! Our housekeeper, Celia, must have come along; there was a section out in the main body of the Pullman car—Celia below with another sister and one of us in the upper berth? Well, it would have been no trick at all for two of us to occupy an upper.

At any rate we were aboard at 9pm, presumably asleep when the train started gliding out of the station at midnight. Don't you believe it! The train always started off very carefully—no jerk—but when the couplings had extended and the full drag of the cars was upon the locomotive there was that rush of spinning wheels, of exhausting steam, and the perceptible jerk as the rims took hold again and the chuff-chuff resumed its measured beat. Asleep? Not likely! We watched our progress out of the station, past the warehouses, over the Mississippi River—and then, with the farmland stretching away, asleep.

Each passing train revived us. A crossing with the dopplered bell ringing caught our attention. The incessant fan might briefly bemuse our questing ears. But nothing was more arresting than a station stop. Abrupt silence. Sights to be seen, people walking about, doing their customary things as though there were no enormously important train standing at their backs. If you stood straight up and on tiptoes you could look out the clerestory (provided the screen were not too dirty) and scoop in the scene. One time it looked right back at me! I recoiled in panic—nothing had prepared me for this large clown on the circus poster impudently staring at all passing trains. No matter what was out there, there was no awakening that was not enhanced by the gleaming mahogany of the fittings within the Pullman.

One of the treats of the trip was the morning visit to the men's lavatory, this of course when my brother and I were old enough to be traveling in a section, possibly alone. Then we took our toothbrushes and paste, often having to wait till a basin should be vacated by a man finished with the tedious job of lathering and razoring his face in the pitching car. We braced ourselves manfully, riding the bucking platform, trying not to have to hold on, but above all not to collide with one of the men. I at least perceived myself as unwelcome since I had no beard to tame before we came to our morning destination. All these men were hurrying against the urgency to look present-able before the train pulled into the station.

The ritual of detraining involved being in the aisle when the porter came through for that redundant whisking off. Bear in mind he had had our shoes from under the berth and had shined them to a fare-ye-well during the night. The brooming was invitation to give a tip. Sometimes Mother would give something for all of us but when we were older we were given the quarter apiece and what I did was to hand it over, not after I'd been whisked, but as we stepped off the train past the porter, who assisted us with our luggage. He was usually pleasant enough, though he might have been tired at the end of the trip and not tolerant of youthful shenanigans. I fancied he glowered at me after brushing me down, figuring I was taking this VIP treatment for free, and I thinking he'd wronged me in so postulating, for see, here I came through with my munificent, adult-type tipping and didn't he feel bad about doubting me?

Arrived at Detroit Fort Street Station, we collected our "carry-on" luggage and made off to the next leg of our happy pilgrimage. This, hopefully, was to the steamer dock at the foot of Woodward, where the *Tashmoo* waited for a 9am sailing. Destination? All together: "Port Huron!" I'm not sure how we got to the dock. Must've been by cab. Perhaps by levitation . . . or streetcar. It wasn't far and not a one of us would have gulped at walking it.

Later, alas, our options expanded. We could somehow: a) pick up the Interurban rail car, or b) go to the Grand Trunk Station and take the train up. These options landed us in Port Huron either, respectively, a) in the center of Military Street down-town, or b) at 24th Street, the Grand Trunk Station. Not fully Up North—but the *Tashmoo*, gliding into the White Star Dock at the foot of Grand River Avenue, definitely delivered us Up North. Usually a grand parade of arrivals and their luggage proceeded from the St. Clair River dock up the four blocks to Huron Avenue, where the streetcar was to be boarded. And from there, on this pitching, squealing, four-wheeled Toonerville Trolley out to Stop 19, never mind the interminable wait as we were switched to the side to let the returning trolley pass. Stop 19, right behind Grandmother's cottage, 4914 Gratiot Beach—and don't stop at the cottage, get your toes into beautiful Lake Huron first thing.

One trip I recall particularly. I was old enough to be embarrassed. Kind, simple-hearted Celia was in charge of this draft, and we did the whole "right" trip, on the Wabash, the *Tashmoo*, the trolley and all. Celia shared our passion for Going Up North, right down to her toes. We discounted her romantic life, but strangely she allowed herself to be beguiled by a salesman on the exciting steamer trip up the river. I could smell illegal alcohol on her breath (this was during Prohibition), and sense her barely suppressed excitement appropriate to Going Up North. But there was something beyond that. After we'd settled ourselves on the trolley bench and were jouncing toward the cottage, Celia could not be dissuaded from singing over and over, *O Me Mither and Fither were Oirish, Me Mither and Fither were Oirish, Me Mither and Fither were Oi-riissssssshh . . . and I am Oirish Stew.*

The Fleeting Days of Summer

What was it about resorts that beckoned and beguiled and charmed? Relaxation, yes, but perhaps what that really meant was the chance to live in the moment, freed (if only temporarily) of the "must do's" that burdened life at home. That luxury, simple but profound, and rare in our lives, provided at least part of the great draw no matter where the resort. As everywhere, so at Lake Huron too the setting enhanced the delight—even relief—of living life in the moment: the limitless horizon of the lake, encouraging one to dream; the entrancing moods of the water; the glorious midwestern clouds; the wind through the elms and cottonwoods and maples; the birdsong at dawn; the sunrise and moonrise across the water; the passing parade of ships. Life in a humble wooden cottage, its porch inviting one to tarry, heightened the senses and made one savor the gifts of nature in a way one didn't so much back home. All together, the chance to ponder the simple things in life relatively unencumbered by the cares of the world kept vacationers flocking back, season after season.

And so, if the magic had done its job, and it usually did, your heart ached when September rolled around and you had to leave behind both the beautiful shores of the lake and the carefree days of summer, to face the daily grind once again. For the contemplative sojourner, summer vacation could seem a metaphor for life itself: beginning, blooming, and ending much too soon. Never mind that the potent magic of vacations lies in their fleeting nature. Like World's Fairs, their very transitoriness makes them special.

But that didn't help the pain at vacation's end.

> At Huronia Beach the breezes are becoming boisterous, and cottagers are regretfully packing sand- and sun-worn effects into their boxes for the return trip. The Windermere Hotel closed last week. (September 18, 1889)

> On the Huronia register the suggestive sentences appear: "Aug. 31, summer has gone; Sept. 1, fall has come again." (September 4, 1897)

> A pathetic incident occurred at the Windermere on Friday afternoon. Mrs. J. H. Harrigan and children, of Detroit, have been guests at the hotel for the past month and on Monday they left. One of the children, a boy of about eight summers, cried as if his heart would break at the thought of leaving the beach where he had spent so many happy moments. He at first objected to

going but using a method of persuasion that only mothers have, he consented to go. (August 8, 1903/H)

The charming summer girl with her dainty frocks and her winning ways is no more till another year. (September 5, 1903/H)

The first week in September at the beach brings with it many a reluctant sigh for the summer that has passed, and slowly and sadly swimming suits are packed, tennis rackets are put aside and toys and bicycles are tucked away for the homeward trek to the city. The exodus from Gratiot beach this week will be heavy. (September 6, 1934)

If you rented at Huronia you could just pack up and leave, but cottage owners at Gratiot had to prepare their cottages for the winter months ahead. Closing chores took days to complete in that era before modern fabrics meant you didn't have to hide drapes and blankets from moths and mice, and electric vacuum cleaners made spring cleanup a cinch. In addition, boats and benches had to come up from the beach. Screens had to come off windows and doors and head into storage, replaced by heavy wooden shutters to protect the cottage over the long winter. Transportation had to be secured and trunks packed.

Ada Greene's diary brimmed each autumn with closing chores:

Went to town to pay bills etc. Clark & Theodore put shutters on cottage in A.M. & Agnes & I with Theodore finished inside in P.M. Clark varnished porch, part of ceiling. — Finished trunk in A.M., went to town, bank etc. in P.M. After supper worked till midnight in cottage, shutters on all but back door, water turned off, suitcases packed, boat in house. — Washed some curtains & doilies. In P.M. put poison down — Called at neighbors', also at Uncle Brown's; he & Aunt Charlotte leave tomorrow on 3:00 train. Finished trunk after supper. — Bright day with lake breeze,

air fine, but almost too busy to enjoy it. Trunk left by trolley
for Detroit at 7:30. Will stopped off water, & we did the final
things towards closing, leaving Beach at 4:20 & Port Huron on
5:35 trolley. Found trunk at D&C dock in Detroit & took boat
for Cleveland. (September 22 and 30, 1911; October 25, 1912;
September 16 and 17, 1915/ADGdiary)

Given the potent combination of end-of-season chores, angst at leaving the
cottage vacant for months, and heartache at bidding farewell to summer,
moody despondency loomed near at hand when closing a beloved cottage,
and emotions could run high.

The second floor is practically ready to leave. Of course my
clothes have to come out of there and the bedclothes be put
away. The bedclothes can't be put away until the last morning,
though. We haven't anyone as yet to put on the shutters but I'll
try to get someone tomorrow. Gee, but I do dread this closing
the cottage with Mother around. She stews over things so. To be
sure, her cottage never had mice nor mildewed beds or bedding
nor much else wrong with it, but it is very trying to her and to
the person who has to work with her. (September 17, 1926/AGB)

On the other hand, mothers who endured weeks of separation from their
husbands in order to manage the cottageful of kids might look forward to
the end of vacation, at least occasionally.

I have wanted you so much lately. Sometimes I rebel and swear
I won't do this each summer. It's too hard on me and I have not
a doubt that it's harder on you. Lots of love to my sweetheart.
(August 5, 1924/AGB)

The more mature cottagers were philosophical about leaving:

The nicest of summers and the best of vacations are bound
to come to an end. Happy is he with a home to which he can

return. So I have reveled in my long stay at the Beach and am
content to be home again and back on the job. (September 10,
1944/TPB)

The glories of the Michigan summer beguiled many a resorter into dream-
ing that life would be perfect if only he or she didn't have to leave:

As always the beach holds plenty of attraction for this member
of the Brookes clan. Would that my work or destiny decree that I
be stationed in Port Huron for good. (August 20, 1944/TPBJr)

But the cold realities of Lake Huron in winter would've quickly doused the
dream, and made the dreamer realize that only by leaving the idyll could
he or she live it again, the next summer. Absence and anticipation rekindled
the flame.

*Empty, snowed-in cottages at the southern tip of
Gratiot Beach, January 1911.*

Chapter 10
The Muse Strikes ... Out?

The joys of summertime along the lake inspired amateur poets and authors to try their hand at capturing in words the passions in their heart.

The Beach ABC's

Seventeen-year-old Mary Dean of Cincinnati, daughter of pioneer Gratiot resorter Elizabeth Dean, read her poem aloud at the entertainment in the nearly brand-new Huronia Dining Hall on Saturday evening, July 17, 1886. Into it Miss Dean wove names of vacationing families, making enough of a splash to appear in the Port Huron newspaper two days later.

> A is for *Armstrong* of Sunday night fame,
> B is for *Baldwin*, there are five of that name,
> C is for *Callendar*, we don't know what year,
> D is for *Dean* of Gratiot, quite near.
>
> E is for *Elwood*, our fisherman bold,
> F is for *Finney* and *Finn*, we're told,
> G is for *Gratiot*, just on through the gate,
> H is for *Hall*, no breakfast if late.
>
> I is for *Ives*, they're not here as yet,
> J is for *Jolly*, that's us you may bet,
> K is for *Kitchen*, it's just in the rear,
> L, *Lemonade*, one lemon all year.
>
> M is for *Miller*, Detroit and Kentuck,
> N, *Nanki-Po*, who swam like a duck,

Up North

O is for *Onions*, sure don't you know,
P is for *Penney* and his big Tally-ho.

Q is for *Quacks*, for which we've no need,
R is for *Races*, the girls always lead,
S is for *Sheldon*, *Smith*, *Siebert*, and *Sand*,
T is for *Table*, the best in the land.

U is for *Unity*, all here together,
V is for *Variety*, in rainy weather,
W is for *Ward*, the last in the row,
X is for Something, but what we don't know.

Y is for *Young*, *Marcus* his name,
From Port Huron we hear that he came,
Zealous, in all things the people to please,
Now you have heard the "Beach ABC's."

Sunday at the Windermere

(June 27, 1896; anonymous verse)

O, an evening at the beaches,
Underneath the sky of June,
Is a season when the senses
Are themselves in perfect tune;
When the brain swims with a vision,
Brighter far than ever shone,
And the heart swells with a feeling
Of delight before unknown.

Oh New York!

In 1971 longtime Gratiot resorter Clark Greene, my grandmother Agnes's younger brother, copied out his poem by hand with the note, "Original composed around 1916 when I first went to work in New York City. Discovered by writer 55 years later."

> *With apologies to Rudyard Kipling and his poem "On the Road to Mandalay."*
>
> By the old lake shore at Gratiot, looking lazy at the "sea"
> There's a peaceful little cottage and I know it waits for me.
> For the wind is off the ocean and the steamers seem to screech
> "Come you back, you New York dweller, come you back to
>   Gratiot Beach."
>
> With the early(?) breakfast over and the hole dug in the ground,
> I used to get the Evinrude and evinrude around.
> With the chug, chug, chug behind me and the tiller in my hand
> I'd sit and watch the changing lights upon the water grand.
> Changing lights upon the lake and the passing steamer's wake
> And a visit to the lightship just for old times' sake.
>
> But all that's shoved behind me far away and out of reach
> And there ain't no busses running from 5th Avenue to the Beach.
> And I'm learning here in New York what everybody tells,
> When you've heard the West a-callin' why you don't heed noth-
>   ing els'.
> No you don't heed nothing els' but them spicy "norther" spells
> And the sunshine and the pine trees and 'specially meal-time bells.

Up North

I'm sick of wasting leather on these gritty paving stones
And the dark and dismal subway wakes the shivers in my bones.
Though I hear a million people saying "Greatest in the land,"
And they speak in awe of Broadway, what do they understand?
Law, what do they understand? Crowds and crush on every hand.
I've a sweeter, greener vision of a cleaner, cheaper land.

Ship me somewhere's west of New York where they've lots of
    "pep and go,"
Where they keep the ten commandments and a guy can save
    some "dough,"
For the chapel bell is calling and I can hear the lake –
Aw shucks! It's the alarm clock and now I'm wide awake.

On Guard

By Gratiot resorter Mary Alice Finney (1876–1962), daughter of early Gratiot resorter Jared W. Finney of Detroit.

At night when I am still awake,
I hear the boats out on the lake
Speak passing signals, each to each,
In ordered, friendly, shipping speech!

If calm the lake or storm winds blow,
It's comforting for me to know
That someone else is there awake,
Keeping watch upon our lake.

My Heritage

By Caryl Jane Finney Fetters Smith (1912–2000), niece of the above poet, and denizen of Gratiot Beach every summer of her life.

> The ghosts of many glorious years gone by
> Have always made my happy summers fly,
> Lake Huron's blue 'neath turquoise tinted skies,
> White sands, ground slowly, sloping here and then again to rise.
>
> Oh Gratiot Beach, my own, my dear delight,
> In all the world to me no happier sight.
> Scene of my healing if I'm sad or ill,
> Place where I go in search of God's own will.
>
> Troubled in mind or heavy be my heart,
> To my dear hideaway I quickly start.
> The sun, the wind, the rain, the waves, the lake,
> Work quickly all and all my troubles take.
>
> Each in their time, I love them all—and then,
> I am my own, my happy self again.
> It seems—of all of us—'tis only I,
> I and my very own are left. May all of them enjoy
> My love, that deep within their hearts,
> Our house at Gratiot Beach will too, to them impart
> A sense of peace throughout the year, our tiny bit of sod,
> Windswept, sun-tanned, and very close to God.

Up North

A Summer Incident: A Story of Love at the Lake Huron Beaches

Tsk-tsk, what *wouldn't* those Cincinnati people do when they got to the Windermere Hotel? (July 27, 1895; short story by F. C. Buzzell)

Everything put on a new aspect after Nora came.

For weeks the same dull monotony had continued at the Windermere, until in spite of the pleasant surroundings of this charming resort, even those who had come here purely for rest and quiet began to wish that something might happen to change the course of events, and instill new life into the gloom which enveloped the place. To be sure there was amusement enough, such as it was. The guests might find pleasure in the daily plunge in the surf, or walk along the broad stretch of sand and watch the ever changing panorama of steamers and sailing vessels as they came up into the lake from the river, and fixed their course for the long pilgrimage up the "unsalted seas."

Then, too, there was the mile of promenade along the front of the cottages at Huronia Beach, where one might chat and gossip with people from all over the country. If this proved too exciting for the visitors, and they pined for something more quieting and solemn, they might go over into Lakeside Cemetery, nearby, and read the epitaphs on the tombstones, and ponder the uncertainties of life.

The people who came here for the summer months were not the butterflies of the fashionable world, with nothing to recommend them but their money. Some of them were rich enough, but the larger number were well-to-do people of the world, belonging to the professional and mercantile classes, who sought out this picturesque spot because it was completely isolated from the ultra-fashionable world, where everything glitters with

194

Huronia's crosswalk on the lake side of the cottages encouraged mingling. Postcard, ca. 1912.

a false and deceitful lustre. Occasionally the "summer girl" would come and linger for a day or two, and then suddenly disappear to make room for the staid-mannered schoolteacher with the unreadable face and the ever-present spectacles. No wonder it was dull, and it is not at all surprising that the denizens began to long for just a little change in the order of things.

Then Nora came. One day the electric car stopped at the Windermere, and among the arrivals was a young woman with a bright, pretty face, and lithe, graceful figure, who would attract attention anywhere. She was quiet and reserved in manner, and did not appear to notice that her advent into this proxy corner of the world had occasioned any curiosity; but it had.

"At last, a pretty girl! I wonder who she can be?" remarked George Mills, a fine-looking man of thirty-five, as he lifted his eyes from the novel he was reading and turned toward his companion.

"How should I know?" answered the one addressed, as he turned his eyes toward the new arrival. "If I am a judge of character, she is just as good as she looks," he remarked as he quietly resumed his reading.

Inside of three days everybody knew Nora. That is, they knew her name was Nora Brown, of Cincinnati, for that was what the hotel register said. More than that they were not supposed to know. At summer resorts people live in the present and the future, not in the past. One thing they were all sure of: no woman with such a face could be anything else but pure and good. Everybody liked her—they couldn't help it. Occasionally she would appear sad, but oftener her charming laugh and buoyant spirits would dissipate the gloom, and make all feel that their little world was all the brighter for her coming.

The days sped on, the monotony had disappeared, and there was more real sunshine about the place than there had been all summer. Even the children noticed the change, and welcomed the innovation.

Of course everybody thought Nora charming, even George Mills, austere man of the world, became interested in her, and determined to win her, if he could.

Harry Stone had also been attracted to her from the first, but made no rash resolves. He would cultivate her acquaintance and drift with the tide. No two men could have been more opposite in character than George Mills and Harry Stone. The former was an accomplished man of modern society, who had seen life in all its phases. He had tasted its sweets and its bitterest dregs. To him the chief aim in life was to bury the past, and live in the present. Successful in business, he could not admit that he could be unsuccessful in any other undertaking. Selfish in the extreme, he lived only to gratify his own desires, regardless of the effect it might have on others. He was cold-blooded and cruel, but he hid it under an impenetrable mask of decency and respectability.

Harry was a man of entirely different type. Strong, manly and honest, he gained and held the confidence and respect of all.

He had not been spoiled by coming in touch with the selfishness and greed of mammon, and his heart was pure and clean. Naturally modest, he was strongly handicapped in a race where, unfortunately too often, through the blindness of woman, the prize is given to the one who least deserves it.

To win Nora was a greater task than George Mills had antici-pated. She had not encouraged him in any way, and her manner had always been frank but circumspect. However, she was only human, and she doubtless felt gratified to receive the homage which all women expect, and are disappointed if they do not receive. He went to work with a will, and by degrees began to draw her to him. He was an artist in his way, and his skill in flattery and attentions soon began to have its effect. Slowly but surely he drew the fetters around her heart, until at last, before she half realized it, she was Love's prisoner.

And yet, sometimes she wondered that her heart did not go out to Harry. One was as attractive as the other, and in many ways Harry was the superior of George. Her woman's heart told her that he was the better of the two, but by that inexplicable, mysterious reasoning of womankind, the same through all the ages, her love went to the one least worthy.

George Mills's path was not smooth and easily traveled. At times there were obstacles in the way, but they were easily brushed aside. What would have turned Harry away was as noth-ing to him. He had set out to win her, and he had succeeded. No wonder he felt elated.

Things now drifted back into their original rut. The monotony again became oppressive. What else could be expected? Cupid had taken captive the one who could brighten up things and drive away ennui. A girl in love is dead to her surroundings and all the world. It has always been that way.

One morning when George was absent Nora went out to their trysting place, a sequestered spot on the lake shore, where she might be alone to dream, as women in love are prone to do. She noticed a letter on the sand, and picking it up, found it addressed to George. It had been opened, and had probably been dropped accidentally by him the evening before. It had a scent of violets, and bore the impress of a woman's hand. Her curiosity was aroused. She knew it was wrong, but she could not resist the temptation to read it. George had never told her any thing about his people, except to mention his mother and sister, and woman-like, she was anxious to learn more of them. The letter was surely from one of them—probably the sister. After some hesitation she opened the letter, glanced carelessly at the superscription, and read, "My Dear Husband!"

Nora was shocked and terribly disappointed. She did not faint as most "resort girls" would do under such trying circumstances, but anyone who could have seen her then would have felt pity for the innocent girl. She was dazed for a moment, and every-thing, which up to that time had looked so bright and cheerful, put on a sombre hue, as she realized that she had been duped. One moment she would give way to tears, followed by angry flashes from her eyes, which boded no good to her false lover when they should meet again.

When George returned to the hotel and found Nora absent, he knew where to find her, and when he reached her side he knew that something had happened. Nora's face was ashen pale, and her eyes flashed with a startling brilliancy. Looking him steadily in the eye, she said: "Wretch! Do not dare to touch me! Go back to the wife you have neglected. You have been untrue to her and false to me! Of all the despicable men in the world, you are the lowest and basest! A man who would win a woman's heart, only to break it, should be execrated by all mankind." He attempted to say something, but she would not listen. "Leave me, I never want to hear your treacherous voice again! Your glance is poison, your presence contamination!"

Without a word of explanation he left her, and returned to the hotel.

Faint and disgusted, Nora was left alone with her own bitter thoughts. For hours she scarcely moved, and it was in this condition that Harry found her.

The next morning the guests were all grieved to learn that Nora was seriously ill. The doctor diagnosed the case as nervous prostration, and when questioned as to her prospects of recovery, shook his head. For several days she remained about the same, and then commenced to improve.

In the meantime George Mills had departed. Harry still remained and kept the sick room bountifully supplied with flowers.

One night the sufferer felt more despondent than usual. She was able to be up and dressed, but her loneliness seemed to oppress her. As the hours sped on she became melancholy and half delirious. She sat by the window and listened to the moaning of the storm without. Every breaker struck the beach with a sullen roar, and dashed the spray in clouds of mist against the window panes. It was two o'clock in the morning when she resolved to end it all. Her mind had given way under the strain.

No one saw her as she emerged from the room, enveloped in a white cloak, and glided like a spectre down the long hallway. The sleepy porter failed to notice the graceful form as it came floating down the great stairs and disappeared through the main entrance. A gust of wind nearly swept her feet from under her, as she reached the long walk which led to the water. Down the planks she darted, unconscious that she was being followed by a gentleman who had seen her rushing from the hotel. As she was about to take the fatal plunge, she was grasped by a pair of strong hands, and drawn into the embrace of — her husband.

Mr. Brown had come in on the one o'clock train, and had arrived at the Windermere just in time. He never learned what had caused a recurrence of his wife's old trouble—a mania for "self-destruction."

Mr. and Mrs. Brown left for Cincinnati on the morning train.

Epilogue

As America's industrialization proceeded apace between 1870 and World War I, the upper reaches of the middle class, in St. Louis as around the country, found themselves with the money and the leisure to leave home for estival escapes that previously only the wealthy could afford. Huronia and Gratiot beaches typified this new penchant for Americans taking a summer vacation at a resort—and also typified the rush by towns or regions possessing natural beauties to cash in on the tourist boom. Build the resorts and the vacationers will come, seemed to be the guiding light. They certainly did come to Huronia and Gratiot.

Both resorts featured the cottages and cottage-like hotels typical of that emerging social phenomenon, the middle-class summer resort: structures built unpretentiously of wood, offering reasonably priced holidays in an attractive setting, away from the heat and tumult of cities, rife with opportunities for play if one had youngsters, or social engagement for the adults, if one so chose—and all within relatively easy reach of great metropolises.

So the pattern of summering at Port Huron emerged and repeated itself season after season from 1880 through 1917. The country's entry into World War I in that year, however, brought unanticipated changes to Port Huron's resorts, as it did to so much else. War work quickly appeared alongside the usual summer activities, since it seemed perhaps a little odd to loaf on summer vacation while the country's soldiers were fighting and dying overseas.

> Tuesday morning of each week the ladies of the Windermere hotel congregate in the lobby and living room to sew for the soldiers. Many of the ladies are busy at sewing machines while others are cutting, basting, and knitting. (August 15, 1917)

The last year of the war, 1918, saw the beginning of the end for Huronia Beach. After Marcus Young's death in 1913, his son Milo kept the resort going, but five years later the younger Young ran into unspecified financial difficulties that caused him to default on the $22,000 mortgage his father had taken out on the Beach in 1909. As a result, in August 1918 Milo deeded the property to Stanley McFarland, a Port Huron banker and real estate developer. In the foreclosure sale of the property the following January, Mr. McFarland paid off Milo's mortgage debt and took over Huronia Beach. For the first time in the resort's thirty-nine summers, the Young family was out of the picture at Huronia.

As soon as he acquired it, Mr. McFarland wasted no time in trying to unload his new property, by selling individual lots to private parties for building year-round homes. While preparing the sale, however, Mr. McFarland opened Huronia Beach for one last hurrah that summer of 1919, the country's first vacation season since the Great War had ended. The pent-up

HURONIA BEACH

Has been sub-divided and is now offered for sale in

Fifty and One-Hundred Foot Lots

This choice property will be adequately protected by building restrictions. The only beach property drained by city sewers. City water mains on every lot. Many of our citizens will buy and establish all year-around residences.

Full particulars on request

Stanley W. McFarland

16 White Block   Phone 513

The end in sight for Huronia Beach. May 16, 1919.

demand of the war years made for good business, and Huronia filled up with renters as always, just as though there were nothing unusual in the air.

Certainly the beach gossip columns that summer blissfully ignored the impending disaster for Huronia, not mentioning at all that the 1919 season promised to be Huronia's last. The usual summer reporting of Who's Where and With Whom went on as always. Ominous news items appeared else-where in the paper, however, when the resort's new owner divided Huronia Beach into twenty-four lots for sale. It seemed to be a hot item:

> The Huronia beach property purchased by Stanley W. McFarland
> to the north and south of the canal is being platted, but has
> been practically sold out, it taking but one day to close out the
> entire beach stretch. (June 21, 1919)

Must've been a gloomy holiday for resorters that summer, knowing the place was slated for demolition as soon as they cleared out at the end of the season.

In mid-September 1919 the *Port Huron Times Herald* announced Mr. McFarland's public auction of all furnishings in the Huronia cottages and dining hall. From the auction listing we get a picture of the mountain of artifacts a summer resort of the era needed, including, among many other items, 400 feather pillows, 700 pillow slips, 80 wire-spring cots with mat-tresses, 40 iron baby beds with mattresses, 150 dressers, 125 commodes, 80 mirrors, 100 lamps and chimneys, and 60 galvanized slop pails.

On the heels of the auction of personal property, Mr. McFarland held a second auction, of the nine now-empty Huronia cottages north of the canal. Good chance to buy a house cheap, if you could cart it off site within thirty days of the sale. What with the city's population having doubled since 1910, just when the war hindered construction, Port Huron needed housing, and several Huronia cottages found new life as modest year-round homes off the beach. As for the Huronia site itself, a handful of wealthy townsfolk bought up the lots in batches of two or three, building grand homes where the hum-ble Huronia cottages had once stood.

Looking south from the canal footbridge on August 20, 1920, not a cottage was standing at Huronia the summer after the resort closed.

Coming as it did directly on the heels of the closure of Huronia Beach, the burning of the Windermere Hotel made summer 1920 a time of loss for those who knew and loved both. Now empty sand—or worse, charred ruins—stood where forty years of summertime joy had reigned. Agnes Brookes recorded the dismal scene at deserted Huronia with her camera on August 20, 1920. Eight days later, the Windermere burned. Bewildered at the double blow, she poured her heart out to Theodore some two weeks after the hotel went up in smoke:

> The burning of the Windermere on top of the abolishing of Huronia has so changed this place that I don't feel that I ever want to see it again. Of course as long as Mother and Father come up here there will always be the desire to be with them but the place itself has lost its attraction. (September 5, 1920/AGB)

Agnes quickly recovered her love for Lake Huron, returning for forty more summers, but the merciless dispatch of Huronia and flaming demise of the

Left: Ex-Huronia cottage #4 moved across the road to its new site in 1920. Below: Same cottage remodeled into a year-round home, 1922.

Windermere proved prophetic. The world had changed. Even without mortgage default or fire, both resorts would have fallen over the ensuing decades to the rise in operating costs that made a summers-only enterprise challenging at best, utterly impractical at worst. And quite apart from the economics, both Huronia and the Windermere lacked modern amenities that vacationers would come to expect soon enough. Add in the changing tastes in vacationing as the twentieth century progressed, given the increasing ease of distant travel by car or plane, plus the growing number of working mothers with restricted vacation time, and one can see how traditional summer resorts faced bleak prospects. Gratiot Beach with its privately owned cottages carried on, but along with other resorts in the decades since the 1920s nearly all of its cottages have given way to year-round homes.

To sum up what summer resorts such as Huronia and Gratiot have meant to countless folk over the decades since 1880, one could turn to the colorful obituary of Marcus Young in the *Port Huron Times Herald* of August 18, 1913:

> It is not given to many men to have their dreams come true in life, particularly that of a dream city, where thousands of people would flock from various corners of the world to have their annual frolic. But Marcus Young built better than most men. He had serious difficulties to overcome but with the same energy, persistence and hard work that has characterized every year of his active life, he kept on building. Today Marcus Young could stand in the midst of his dream city with a smile of accomplishment and contentment on his face. Before his vision stretched the vast expanse of Lake Huron's crystal water. . . . On the broad verandas of the neat cottages are happy and contented fathers and mothers, smiling youths and maidens, bubbling over with the joy and happiness of life. Away from the sweltering streets of the city, breathing in the clear, cool air of the lake and bathing in its refreshing waters, every passing week is a year added to their life.
>
> And all this was made possible by one man—the man standing on the beach. It is a great thing to have accomplished something big but it is a greater thing to have added to the sum of human happiness.
>
> The dream city of Marcus Young is no longer a dream. It is a real throbbing, busy, happy scene of joy and peace. Marcus Young built from a big idea and he built with a big heart.

Your vision gave plenty of others the chance to dream, Mr. Young.

Appendix A
How to Spend Your Vacation

Family letters and diaries, and the Port Huron newspapers' beach columns, record the range of social activities cottagers pursued at Huronia and Gratiot. Among the pleasant ways to pass the time, one favorite reigned as king of summer nights:

> Corn roasts and marshmallow roasts are all the rage on the beaches and every night many illuminations can be seen along the shore. Clustered around the fire are young people watching with an eager eye the roasting of the corn. An impromptu program always accompanies every "Roast." (September 1, 1900/H)

Of the myriad activities gleaned from those sources, and listed below, along with evening "roasts" or bonfires perhaps only lolling in the lake and strolling the sidewalk have endured as perennial favorites from the days before television and then computers eroded the time people spend in one another's company.

Concerts, shows, and lectures
    Chautauqua (downtown Port Huron)
    evening concert at Huronia
    kinetoscope show
    "Living Pictures" exhibition (*tableau vivant*)
    minstrel show, at Huronia
    stereopticon show

Appendix A

Dances
    a "german" (cotillion)
    cakewalk, at Windermere
    "hop" held at the dancing pavilion
    masquerade ball

Food preparation & eating
    bake a cake
    eat orange ice
    make butter
    make candy
    make fudge
    make taffy
    pick grapes and make grape jelly

Games & activities, indoor
    card games
      Drive-whist (progressive whist)
      Rook
      "42"
    listen to the Victrola
    spelling bee, or "match" (or backwards spelling match)
    Spin the Plate
    Up Jenkins

Games & activities, outdoor
    auto ride
    baseball game (between Huronia & city or Gratiot
      Beach teams, or between Huronia & the men of the
      Life Saving Station)
    call on neighbors
    croquet
    golf
    hayride

horseback ride

lie in hammock

peanut hunt

ride bicycles

ride in a launch

row on the lake (or midnight row)

swim in the lake (or midnight dip)

take a walk (or moonlight stroll on the beach)

tennis

Parades—join in or watch

baby parade

waist parade (wearing colorful blouses)

Parties

a "Chocolate"

baby party

backward party

beach party

  corn roast

  marshmallow roast

  melon roast

  weenie roast

dinner (fancy) at St. Clair Inn

donkey party

farmer's party

hare and hound party

hat party

poverty hop or poverty ball

sheet and pillow case party

spider web party

streetcar party

taffy pull

Appendix A

      a "tea"

      tackie party

      thimble party

      trolley party

      Welsh rarebit party

Reading

      read a book

      read letters aloud

Religious activities

      Bible conference

      song service (evenings, at chapel)

      Sunday morning services

      Sunday School

Sewing

      sew and cut out

      hold a "Fancywork"

Writing

      keep your diary

      write letters

Appendix B
Where Were They From?

On occasion the summer editions of the Port Huron newspapers published lists of the families sojourning at Huronia, Gratiot, or the Windermere Hotel. The lists provide names of resorters, yes, but also show the cities from which they hailed. Though the lists are far from unimpeachably reliable sources, still they allow us to track, in a general way, changes over time in the demographic origin of the resorters.

The first such list we have, from 1890, tallied cottagers at Huronia Beach only. At that early date Ohio cities led far and away, with Columbus on top. One suspects that arrivals later that summer may have tipped the scales in Cincinnati's favor, however, given that Cincinnati in 1890 boasted three times the population of Columbus.

July 17, 1890 Huronia Beach 30 families	
Columbus, O.	14 (47%)
Cincinnati, O.	4
Detroit, Mich.	4
Dayton, O.	3
Port Huron	1
Sidney, O.	1
Indianapolis, Ind.	1
Toledo, O.	1
Kansas City, Mo.	1

Two summers later, the *Port Huron Daily Times* of August 5, 1892, listed families at Huronia, Gratiot, and the Windermere Hotel. Arranging the cities of origin according to the number of "hits" at Huronia yields the following table:

Origin of Families	Huronia Beach	Gratiot Beach	Windermere Hotel
Cincinnati, O.	22	-	3
Columbus, O.	6	3	3
St. Louis, Mo.	5	1	3
Akron, O.	4	-	-
Detroit, Mich.	4	7	4
Chicago, Ill.	3	1	1
Port Huron	3	4	-
Quincy, Ill.	3	-	-
Dayton, O.	1	2	2
Springfield, O.	1	-	-
Cottage Hill, O.	1	-	1
Hudson, O.	1	-	-
Toledo, O.	1	-	-
Aurora, Ind.	1	-	-
Evansville, Ind.	1	-	-
Adrian, Mich.	1	-	-
Lockport, N.Y.	-	-	1

As of 1892, then, Cincinnati led the pack as the hometown of families summering at Huronia Beach, in that era at the cusp of Huronia's tremendous growth. More populous than Detroit in 1890, Cincinnati could easily send vacationers via convenient railroad connections to Port Huron. No doubt the first to come (whether through friends or advertising) then spread the word among fellow denizens of the Ohio River metropolis.

Not surprisingly, Detroit and Port Huron led at Gratiot, since these two cities lay much closer to this beach at which families owned cottages rather than rented. The farther away the hometown, the less likely that a family would purchase a cottage; logically these more distant resorters would prefer instead to rent, since the family (or at least Dad) couldn't just pop up to the Beach whenever opportunity struck. Also unsurprisingly, not a single Port Huron family stayed the night at the Windermere Hotel at this time, since these locals could easily return to their homes in town for the night. Plenty of locals would come to the hotel during the day, though, to dine in its restaurant and enjoy its porch and its beach.

The list testifies that Huronia and Gratiot attracted midwesterners overwhelmingly, but not many from the Midwest's greatest metropolis, Chicago. Chicagoans with the wherewithal to do so flocked to Lake Michigan's resorts, since those watering holes required a shorter train or steamer ride from their hometown. Port Huron's resorts still drew primarily from Michigan and Ohio in 1892, as they had when the resorts opened twelve years previously.

The 1892 list also tells us how long the vacationers stayed at Huronia that summer:

Length of stay at Huronia (in weeks)	Number of families
2	1
4	4
6	14
7	1
8	13
9	3
10	7
11	2
12	6

So in this year for which we have data, 1892, 55 percent of the families rented cottages for the period of six to eight weeks. Another 30 percent stayed between two and one-half and three months. Given the effort involved to arrange train and steamer tickets, pack trunks, and undertake the travel, and factoring in the lingering steamy weather back home that one was trying to avoid, it's easy to see why the vast majority of vacationers at Huronia (85 percent of the families there) booked such long vacations. Typically Dad himself remained at home for all but perhaps two weeks of that lengthy time, working, while the rest of the family loafed at Lake Huron.

We don't have similar figures for the Windermere Hotel, but newspaper accounts tell us that there too wealthier patrons might stay not just days, but weeks, or even the entire summer.

As we have seen, by 1900 St. Louis had surged ahead as the number-one supplier of resorters at Huronia, as the nation's fourth-largest city offered plenty of citizens seeking escape from summer sultriness. Looking at the map, one might think St. Louisans would flock to the somewhat closer resorts on Lake Michigan, and plenty did, but the through-train service described in chapter 9 brought many to Lake Huron, and just as conveniently as to northern Lake Michigan. As of 1905, at Huronia Beach:

July 1, 1905 Huronia Beach 46 families	
St. Louis	28 (60%)
Detroit	6 (13%)
Columbus, O.	5
Mt. Clemens, Mich.	3
Port Huron	1
Dallas, Tex.	1
Sedalia, Mo.	1
Memphis, Tenn.	1

After 1910, the emerging metropolis of Detroit began to outstrip all rivals in furnishing resorters for Port Huron's beaches. This is not surprising, since Detroit had entered its boom period triggered by the automobile industry. Detroit's proximity to Port Huron made the latter's resorts a natural choice for Motor City residents.

Among the arriving families at the Windermere Hotel, for the week ending August 14, 1913, Port Huron made a strong showing. Mr. West's expansion of the hotel clearly attracted the locals now, including from nearby Michigan and Ontario towns:

August 14, 1913 Windermere Hotel 93 families	
Detroit	26
Port Huron	22
St. Louis	6
Toledo, O.	5
Flint, Mich.	5
Chicago	4
St. Clair, Mich.	4
Columbus, O.	3
Sarnia, Ont.	2
Austin, Tex.	2
Albion, Mich.	2
Yale, Mich.	2
Indianapolis	1
Ann Arbor, Mich.	1
Lansing, Mich.	1
Monroe, Mich.	1
Imlay City, Mich.	1
Ft. Wayne, Ind.	1
Muskogee, Okla.	1
New York, N.Y.	1
Richmond, Va.	1
London, Ont.	1

The last list we have, of arriving families at Huronia June 25–29, 1915, reflects the expected lead of Detroit even so early in the season that year.

June 25–29, 1915 Huronia Beach 27 families	
Detroit	9
St. Louis	5
Cleveland	5
Greenville, Miss.	3
Little Rock, Ark.	1
New York, N.Y.	1
Toledo, O.	1
Kansas City, Mo.	1
Port Huron	1

St. Louis still gave the Motor City a run for its money at Huronia in late June 1915, as the list shows, while among Ohio cities, surging Cleveland now furnished more cottagers than any other Buckeye town, with Cincinnati and Columbus bowing out completely. The season was yet early, so that arriving families could well have shifted these numbers as the summer progressed, yet still we may safely conclude that booming Detroit by then firmly led the pack at Lake Huron.

By 1919, the beach columns in the summer Port Huron paper corroborate the overwhelming preponderance of Detroiters at all the lakeside resorts, with but a smattering of vacationers from the traditional sources in Ohio and Missouri. The trend only continued when Huronia Beach went out of business that fall, eliminating a major supply of rental cottages, which the more distant vacationers tended to prefer.

St. Louis's reign as Queen of Huronia and Gratiot may have ended, but still when summer dawns, a number of Gateway City residents flock Up North to continue the tradition on Lake Huron shores. And they do it for the same reasons their ancestors did, for what held true then holds true today:

> We get a decided change in weather by coming here. If you
> lived in St. Louis, you'd appreciate Port Huron in the summer-
> time. (September 3, 1936)

Notes

1. Orvar Löfgren, *On Holiday: A History of Vacationing* (Berkeley: University of California, 1999), 147–153.

2. Cindy S. Aron, *Working at Play: A History of Vacations in the United States* (New York: Oxford, 1999), 15–16.

3. Löfgren, *On Holiday*, 134.

4. Löfgren, *On Holiday*, 153.

5. Aron, *Working at Play*, 166.

6. Löfgren, *On Holiday*, 118.

7. Löfgren, *On Holiday*, 164.

8. Nor was pressure let up that winter, as the *Ft. Gratiot Sun* of December 3, 1881, simply and confidently declared on its front page, "Huronia Beach is to be the summer resort the coming summer."

9. Herschel Bouton Lazell, *Michigan Reports: Cases Decided in the Supreme Court of Michigan*, vol. 137 (Chicago: Callaghan, 1906), 423–424.

10. Löfgren, *On Holiday*, 145.

11. For the record, the the first cottages and the Windermere Hotel didn't go up until 1886.

12. Cummings D. Whitcomb, *A Lake Tour to Picturesque Mackinac* (Detroit: Gulley, Bornman & Co., 1884), 54.

13. Personal communication from Robert D. Brookes to author, ca. 1985.

14. RDB Huronia.

15. Aron, *Working at Play*, 115–116.

16. Whitcomb, *A Lake Tour*, 54.

17. My thanks to Dr. Paul Groth, professor of geography and architecture, University of California, Berkeley, for these insights into nineteenth-century hotel plumbing.

18. *Port Huron Daily Times*, July 19, 1886.

19. Löfgren, *On Holiday*, 92.

20. First verse of the hymn whose words were penned by British poet James Montgomery (d. 1854).

21. RDB Huronia.

22. *Port Huron Daily Times*, September 6, 1882.

23. *Annual Report of the United States Life-Saving Service* (Washington: G.P.O., 1908).

24. Lazell, *Michigan Reports*, 424.

25. Helen Ingram, *Three on a Tour* (Detroit: John Bornman & Son, 1895), 49.

26. Anonymous, "Neither Soldier or Sailor," *White Star Magazine* (1918), 41.

27. Jack E. Schramm and William H. Henning, *When Eastern Michigan Rode the Rails* (Glendale, CA: Interurban Press, 1986), 41 and 185.

28. *Official Blue Book*, vol. 4, "The Middle West" (Cincinnati: Automobile Club of Cincinnati, 1916), 160–161.

29. Schramm and Henning, *When Eastern Michigan Rode the Rails*, 142–146.

30. *Port Huron Times Herald*, Blue Water edition, August 1938.

Bibliography

Anonymous. "Neither Soldier or Sailor." *White Star Magazine*, 1918.

Aron, Cindy S. *Working at Play: A History of Vacations in the United States.* New York: Oxford, 1999.

Huronia Beach. Season of 1884. A Family Summer Resort. Brochure in Michigan Room, St. Clair County Public Library, Port Huron, MI.

Ingram, Helen. *Three on a Tour.* Detroit: John Bornman & Son, for the Detroit and Cleveland Steam Navigation Company, 1895.

Jenks, William L. *St. Clair County, Michigan: Its History and Its People.* Chicago: Lewis, 1912.

Lazell, Herschel Bouton. *Michigan Reports: Cases Decided in the Supreme Court of Michigan.* Vol. 137. Chicago: Callaghan, 1906.

Löfgren, Orvar. *On Holiday: A History of Vacationing.* Berkeley: University of California, 1999.

Schramm, Jack E., and William H. Henning. *When Eastern Michigan Rode the Rails.* Glendale, CA: Interurban Press, 1986.

Whitcomb, Cummings D. *A Lake Tour to Picturesque Mackinac.* Detroit: Gulley, Bornman & Co., for the Detroit and Cleveland Steam Navigation Company, 1884.

Photo Credits

Unless noted below, by page number, photographs are by Agnes Greene Brookes or from her photo albums. Advertisement illustrations dated 1909 or earlier are from the *Port Huron Daily Times*; those dated 1910 or later are from the *Port Huron Times Herald*. Captions identify persons in photographs from left to right.

Brookes, Jean I.: 83, 101, 102, 117, 120

Brookes, Robert D.: 72, 74, 177, 179

Greene, Clark R.: 39, 47, 91, 188

Krummes, Daniel C.: 56 top right, 104 left

Michigan History Room, St. Clair County Library: 25 ("Souvenir History of Port Huron" file); 38 ("Port Huron in Summer" file); 46 ("Windermere" file)

Pesha, Louis James: 52, 124

Unknown photographer: 4, 37 top, 127

Index

Page numbers in *italics* refer to illustrations.